Carol resides in Glasgow, Scotland, where she has lived for most of her life—apart from a brief time spent in England in her youth, where they promptly sent her back for being too cheeky. The youngest of five siblings who all grew up in Glasgow in the 50s, she is no stranger to overcoming adversity in her life.

Didn't Expect That, Did You? is her first published book and the realisation of her desire to share her breast cancer journey in the hope that it helps others going through the same experience in their own lives.

When not writing, she enjoys knitting and reading and having battles of will with her sassy Jack Russell terrier, Wee Jessie. (Wee Jessie occasionally lets her win).

This book is dedicated to my two beautiful daughters, Claire and Laura, who have always been there for me through the bad times and the good, and to my partner, Jim, who has walked this journey with me.

And as always, to my family—it's a Butterly thing (we all know what that means!)

Carol Butterly

DIDN'T EXPECT THAT DID YOU

AUSTIN MACAULEY PUBLISHERS
LONDON * CAMBRIDGE * NEW YORK * SHARJAH

Copyright © Carol Butterly 2025

The right of Carol Butterly to be identified as author of this work has been asserted by the author in accordance with sections 77 and 78 of the Copyright, Designs and Patents Act 1988.

All rights reserved. No part of this publication may be reproduced, stored in a retrieval system, or transmitted in any form or by any means, electronic, mechanical, photocopying, recording, or otherwise, without the prior permission of the publishers.

Any person who commits any unauthorised act in relation to this publication may be liable to criminal prosecution and civil claims for damages.

All of the events in this memoir are true to the best of author's memory. The views expressed in this memoir are solely those of the author.

A CIP catalogue record for this title is available from the British Library.

ISBN 9781037111488 (Paperback)
ISBN 9781037111495 (ePub e-book)

www.austinmacauley.com

First Published 2025
Austin Macauley Publishers Ltd®
1 Canada Square
Canary Wharf
London
E14 5AA

To the fantastic staff at the Beatson Cancer Unit—there are no words that I can say that can properly express how much you have done to support me and my family through this journey. Special thanks to Claire, my breast nurse, who was always there for me at the end of the phone whenever I needed.

This is not a story, as people would say; it's the journey of my path down the scary, unpredictable, winding, and twisting road of emotions and not knowing, what, or who, knows what happens next? When you are told the horrifying words: *Yes, it's cancer*.

It all started one night, sitting watching TV after I had a lovely warm shower, cooried in, as we Scots say, on the big armchair, legs all tucked under, and getting ready to watch a movie. I folded my arms under my arms. Then I felt a small lump and thought to myself, *What is this? Should it be here? Is it part of my arm? Maybe it's an artery, a vein, etc.* I continued to feel around for a wee while, then thought to myself, *No, this shouldn't be here.*

I didn't think, there was no pain from it, I may add, or, from what I could see at that angle, no bruising.

I got up from the chair and asked Jim, my partner who was watching TV with me, to have a look, and to see if he could feel anything. Jim said: 'I'm not sure, Carol, but you know your own body, and if something doesn't feel right, then make an appointment at the doctor's.' Which I did, the very next morning.

I couldn't sleep at all that night, as you can imagine. All sorts of scenarios were going through my mind. First and foremost were my two daughters, Claire and Laura. *What will they do? What will Jim do? What will my sister Nancy do? And also my two brothers, my sister-in-law, and other close members of my family. How could I tell them?* My mind was working overtime. Then I said to myself, *Hang fire a minute, I am jumping the gun, as it's said. This might be nothing, maybe just a milk duct or a cyst.*

I had a cyst years before, when Laura was just a baby— 18 months old. I was sent to see a professor in the Western Infirmary, Glasgow, and I was glad to be told it was just a cyst. All clear.

The next morning, as soon as the doctor's surgery opened, I called to ask for an appointment. I got one for the very next day. The doctor was a locum, a young girl, and after examining me, she said we didn't have to worry too much, as she thought it was what they call a "mouse breast". Personally, I had never heard of this, but she said, 'I'll send you for a mammogram, just to be on the safe side, but there is no hurry. So, I don't want you to worry.'

Easier said than done! But with her reassurance, I felt a lot better about it. So, I went home and waited for the appointment to arrive in the post.

A few days went by, and the letter came. Here it was, my appointment for the mammogram to deal with this so-called *mouse breast.* My appointment was just a few days away, an early morning slot.

On the morning of the mammogram, I got up and had a cuppa tea, as I couldn't eat anything, I was far too nervous, and I felt nauseous. I arrived at the clinic, and my name was called. I noticed, while I was there, that it was quite busy, men and women, of all ages: young, old, in-between. It really struck me, as I never thought the clinic would be as busy as this.

I was there on my own, as Jim, Nancy, and my two daughters were at their work and couldn't get the time off. In a way, I preferred to be on my own, as I was sure there was nothing to worry about, according to my GP. I went into the bay for the procedure, myself and the radiographer, as they are called now.

If you haven't had a mammogram, it can be really uncomfortable. They have to get all of your breast, my left one in this case, onto this flat surface, and tuck in any parts that are hanging over the edge. Sounds very sore and hurtful, and believe me, it is! Then your breast is flattened, yes, flattened, by this other part of the machine, while the radiographer goes over to a desk to take a reading. All the while, your breast is trapped under this contraption, as I called it, for a good few minutes. Seems like a lot longer, believe me.

The relief when she says, 'That's it, I have a good reading,' and then releases the pressure, you have never felt relief like it, honestly. Well, that was my experience of it. So, it was time to get dressed, go home, and wait for the results to be sent out to me.

I went home and just carried on as usual. I was working in Nutmeg at the time, which is a children's retail company. I enjoyed it. It was situated within Morrisons supermarket. I didn't have far to travel, as it was just across the road from my flat.

I had no intentions of having a diary of sorts until I went to the doctor's with the lump in my breast. I came across the wee book in my drawer just the other day, and I had written this in it. I'm not sure what made me write in this wee book, things as they were progressing. I mean, no one suggested it to me. It just happened. I picked it up and just started writing in it. I'm not sure it's a good thing or not, but they, the experts, say that if you write it down, then you're getting it out of your system and not bottling it up. Not sure about that one. Maybe other stuff, but not something as big as this. It's just a wee book that I kept a note of all my shifts in for work.

I received a letter to go for another mammogram, also a scan and a biopsy. Things weren't looking too good at this stage. I kept saying to myself, *This bloody mouse breast is causing a lot of commotion for something we were not to worry too much about!*

Today is the 12th of February, eight days after my 62nd birthday, which, may I say, Jim and the girls made lovely. They got me flowers, cake, a beautifully cooked dinner, and I opened all my gifts. We had a great day. That was the week before.

Today was the day, as I said earlier, for the scan, biopsy, and mammogram. They could not see anything with the mammogram, so they gave me a scan. They saw, on the small monitor, what they said was a growth, so they proceeded with the biopsy to take it out for testing. The biopsy tool looked like a metal gun.

Before that, she injected my breast with a painkiller. At this time, Jim was sitting across from me on a chair in the corner, and he said later that he could see the growth on the small screen. He said it was tiny. The doctor, as we will call her, then proceeded to put the biopsy probe into my breast. She said it goes into the breast, then it will open up and grab the growth. She said she would count to three, then open the grabber. She counted, 'Three,' and I nearly shot up to the roof.

I can take pain; I am not a fearty by any means. I mean, I delivered Laura, my second daughter, without any pain relief, not by choice, but that's how it was on the day. Anyway, Jim nearly jumped out of the chair he was sitting on. She said to me, 'Did you feel that?' I said yes. She apologised and gave me more pain relief. She tried again a few minutes later, and there was no pain, just discomfort. Then she turned to Jim and said, 'Isn't she a brave lady?' Jim agreed with her, and, incidentally, so did I. I got dressed and Jim and I went home to wait.

A few days later, on 15 February 2018, I think, I went to the clinic for my results. I was called into the consultant's room to hear the results of my biopsy. I was there on my own; I think I preferred it that way. I was not really worried, as I had been led to believe this was a minor detail of the breast. I went into the room and was told by the consultant to take a seat. A breast nurse stood by her side at the desk. I tried to read their faces but couldn't. The surgeon turned the monitor towards me and said the words, 'It's cancer.' I looked at the screen, not knowing what I was looking at or looking for. Then she said, 'YOU DIDN'T EXPECT THAT, DID YOU?' I was numb, shocked. I looked at the nurse, and she just nodded her head to agree with the consultant. I don't remember much about those couple of minutes as my brain was foggy. I was just staring into space. I wanted to ask questions, but my mouth wouldn't move, nor would my body, for that matter. Then, before I could say anything, the nurse gave me some leaflets, showed me to the door and said, 'Read these when you get home.' To say I was made to feel like a piece of nothing, I can't even find a word to describe how I felt. Now, I know these surgeons and nurses hear this information about cancer all the time, but they've got to remind themselves that the person receiving it doesn't and should be given time and listened to, not just tossed out the door to deal with it themselves and know not how to condense it, let alone understand what's happening to their body. A bit of empathy, humanity, a few kind words of support, whatever happened to the wee cup of tea? That would have gone a long way. Well, to start with, the surgeon saying to me, 'You didn't expect that, did you?' was, to say the least... well, to be truthful, I did say back to her, 'No, I didn't expect that.' Then I was struck dumb. What had I done to this woman for her to talk to me like this? I should have said something to her, but, of course, I didn't. I left the clinic and went out to the car park. I just got into my car and put the engine on. The radio came on, and the first thing that came on the radio was a Macmillan Cancer advert, typical. I sat there for maybe a few minutes, then I started the engine and drove home. I got home and put the kettle on for a cuppa tea.

Just then, the door opened and Nancy came in. She has keys to my house, so she let herself in. She just stood at the entrance to the living room and said to me, 'How did you get on?' I looked at her and said, 'It's breast cancer.' Her face said everything I was thinking. The next few days were a blur, not taking anything in, just going through the motions and determined to be positive and strong. I hoped everyone around me did the same. Jim came home from work early; he was really upset. His boss sent him home. I was really worried about him; his mind seemed to be wandering; he was thinking too much. He'll handle things his own way.

The next day I went to tell my brother and his wife. I wasn't sure how I was going to do this. I still hadn't told my two daughters, Claire and Laura. It was so hard trying to get them together, as they both lived apart, Claire was in Edinburgh, Laura lived in Abbotsinch. So, I started arranging to get them to my house at the same time, which, believe me, wasn't easy. I would get Claire to my house, then give Laura a call. She would be working late or couldn't make it. Then I would start again. It took me half a dozen tries to get them both together at the same time in my house.

I've just remembered, before all this started, Mark and Elaine, good friends of the family, got engaged. Great night at David Lloyd Centre. Walking home with shoes in hand and Nancy's socks on, my feet were killing me from too much dancing. Jim was affronted, but Nancy and I were just laughing, as you do. It was raining, so my feet were soaked through. I didn't care—again, as you do when you're being silly and maybe had a drink or two. Good night, though. Thanks, Mark.

At last, I got my two daughters together on my sofa, in my house. It was quite late at night. We were all sitting together, and I told them. It was one of the hardest things I ever had to say to them. They both sat quietly and listened until I finished speaking. The questions came one after another, and I answered them as honestly as I could, considering I didn't have all the information.

I must say, they were both brilliant. Strong, supportive, brave. They didn't break down like a pack of cards. They took every word in, tried to understand what was about to happen to me, and to them, of course, because they would be walking that road with me. We all cuddled each other. There were no tears. As I say, I have two of the strongest, most capable, bravest, and most beautiful females I have ever known.

After we cuddled for a while and held onto each other, we said our goodnights. I went to my bedroom and left the two girls together. After a while, I heard them leave the house to go back to their homes.

The next day, it was time to tell my brother and his wife. I hated having to tell them, but what could I do? They had a right to know. I didn't want everyone to know, and my girls didn't know them that well.

Nancy, Jim, and I got in the car and drove to their house. We parked and walked up to the door. All the while, I was saying to myself, *Just leave it until another day. Leave it until next week when we have more information.* But at the same time, I didn't want them hearing the news from someone other than me.

We knocked on their door and Claire, my sister-in-law, let us in. They already had a visitor in the house, so we just sat and chatted about trivial things—weather, holidays, etc. All the while, my stomach was churning over and over.

Once the other visitor left, it was just us. I had a feeling Claire knew we weren't just there for a catch-up. I mean, there were three of us. Usually, I would go on my own to visit Claire and Junior—my brother and sister-in-law. There wouldn't normally be all three of us together.

Anyway, we were chatting away, and Junior was in the kitchen with his grandson. I was sitting on the sofa when Jim leant forward and said to me, 'You need to go in and see Junior. I told him you had got some bad news.'

Now, to say I was angry was an understatement. Then Jim walked out of the room. I was seething, trying to hold my temper and look as normal as possible—very, very hard for me.

The reason why? This was *my* news. This was my news to tell my brother, and to tell him in a way that was comfortable for me, and also not to be too harsh or worrying. It was *my* news, *my* life, what was happening to me and *my* body. It was not Jim's place to decide where or when this should be told to my family. He took that away from me, and I will never, ever forgive him for that. I was really scunnered by what he did.

So, in the end, I had to rush into the kitchen while Junior was on his own and just blurt out the news to him. He just stared at me. It took a while before I saw it click on his face—his youngest sister had breast cancer.

I wanted to crawl out the door, slip under the kitchen rug, be anywhere but there. I can't even remember the actual words I said to him, honestly, but I will never forget the look on his face.

What if, in that moment, I'd changed my mind? The option was all but gone for me. What if I didn't want to tell them until it was all over, whatever needed to be done: operations, follow-up procedures, etc.? That was all taken from my hands.

Thinking back now, I should have taken it into my own hands and dealt with it, instead of being urged to do it the way it was done. It happened that way, and there is no going back now.

We all went into the lounge. Claire made us tea and started asking questions. I didn't have any answers, as I was still waiting for my next appointment to find out if it was serious—or maybe something like fibromyalgia,

The surgeon had mentioned something about going into the side of the breast with what she described as 'keyhole surgery'. They would remove the growth that way, and I would still have my breast. There is a medical term for it, but I can't remember the name.

Jim and I just got on with day-to-day things as best we could. We went for a drive, but no matter where we went, cancer was on my mind 24/7. I am usually a positive, strong, upbeat person, but all I could think about was death—when, where. I mean, nobody knows when, but when you're given *that* word, cancer, you never know how it will affect you until it's said to you. I didn't.

We went to see Claire and Junior. I forgot to take back her soup pot, she brought it at Christmas along with a side of ham. That was a great night. Had a wee wine with Claire, which I always enjoy. And the company, it's not all about the wine, it's the wee chinwag too. The wine helps, ha ha!

I went for an MRI scan this morning—9:15 a.m. By now it must be late February. The last few weeks I've just kept going as best I could. That MRI machine, though—what a racket! I had headphones on, listening to Smooth Radio, but could barely hear the music for the banging. What a horrible, noisy machine.

Afterwards, Jim and I went to Wetherspoons for a bite. Nancy joined us later. You know, I really enjoyed it. It was a great release. I came home, had a wee nap, then watched the Brit Awards. A relaxing evening, the best it could be under the circumstances.

I remember sitting there, trying to get my head around what I was going to say to my girls. Not sure how to approach the rest of this journey, there's no easy way, I know. I hoped I'd get a decent sleep. I'd written it all in my wee book.

I went to Dr Rousse, my GP. I asked her for sleeping tablets. She spoke to me kindly and said, 'You know you're going to be alright. Just promise you won't Google anything.' I felt better after that. She has her own health problems. That's what I meant earlier about compassion. A kind word—just a little empathy—can go such a long way.

Still working at Nutmeg. It is ideal. Keeps my mind off things.

Woke up, though I never really slept. I am reading over what I wrote in my wee book. Thank goodness for wee books, eh? I had actually forgotten half of what I had written down, and reading it brings it all back, just as it happened.

Laura must have stayed over, as she left for work this morning. Claire and I took the dogs for a walk along the canal. Later that evening, Claire, my daughter, got us a takeaway. We watched the TV and then went to bed. She must be staying with me at this time.

Claire and Junior invited us over for dinner, homemade soup and lovely Irish stew, so my wee book says. Junior was reminiscing about old times; we had a good wee laugh. We came home and went to bed. 'Three days to go', it says in my wee book, but for what, I don't know. I can't remember. Maybe the wee book will enlighten me as the pages turn.

I made a casserole this morning, hope it turns out okay. I did some ironing, tidied up, hoovered, the usual. How exciting, eh?

I sat down to finish the rest of my book. I'm near the end and need to buy another one to keep me going, I love reading books. Thinking I might go for a haircut tomorrow.

The casserole was lovely, very tasty. Jim enjoyed it. He even had seconds, so it must have been good.

I still have not finished my book though. I picked it up, but I can't concentrate on it at the minute. I tried watching

Marcella, but I couldn't concentrate on that either. I took half a sleeping tablet and got a fairly good sleep. Still, sometimes I think to myself, why even sleep? You may only have a few sleeps left. Those kinds of thoughts creep in, uninvited.

The weather is supposed to turn really bad—a Siberian wind coming our way, or so they said on the TV. Snow was expected, and I thought I might go for some shopping later if the weather was not too bad. The nurse called to confirm the date for Friday.

The next morning, I woke to find it had been snowing during the night. My wee rescue dog, Jess, a wee Jack Russell Jim and I had got from the rescue centre, needed her morning walk. I popped her woolly coat on, and we headed out. After we got back, I switched on *Good Morning*. Wrong thing to do, as it was all about death and losing loved ones.

I went out shopping with Nancy. Any excuse to get out and take my mind off things. I picked her up from work, and we went to Pets at Home. I also popped into Laura's work to give her an adapter she had left behind at my place.

Nancy and I then went for a KFC, breast of chicken and chips. Why not? Later that night, I came home and made salmon and chips. 'Toffs are careless', as the saying goes.

Ryan (Jim's nephew), Kirsty, and wee Miley came over for a visit. I love their company. We had a good laugh, about Kirsty's hen do in Portugal. We watched the video of the bull ride—what a scream! The girls trying to hang on was pure comedy. Wee Miley is something else.

The following night, it was just Jess and me. I poured myself a wee glass of wine and watched a bit of TV. Jess got bored of me and went to her wee bed. 'I'll go to mine in a minute,' I said to her. Honestly, I am so, so glad I have been writing all this down in my wee book.

The next day brought a full-blown blizzard, the worst I've seen in a long time. Jim fell on his shoulder on his way to work, and Nancy cut her finger when she slipped in the snow. She didn't make it into work. I decided not to go into my shift either. I'll go in tomorrow instead, weather permitting. Claire got sent home from her work too.

I took Jess out earlier. The snow was up to her tummy, and she loved it, until the cold wind came in and we both ran to the door of the flats. Once inside, I wrapped her up in a warm towel to dry her off.

Then I got a text from Gartnavel, tomorrow's appointment is cancelled. I was so disappointed. I really just wanted it over with. Now I have to wait, and I don't know for how long.

I'm due back at work tomorrow, the 4-8 shift, and again on Friday. All the good shifts, eh? Right, it will help take my mind off stuff.

Jim is doing my head in at the minute, not helping whatsoever. We've been snapping at each other's throats lately. Probably the stress. He's in pain with his shoulder, knees, and ankles, but won't go to see a doctor. Taking all sorts of painkillers instead. As if I don't have enough on my plate. If it were me doing that, he'd be having a go. 'Do as I say, not as I do,' eh? Anyway, we will need to get through this the best we can. I just wish he wouldn't be so serious at the time. I'm trying to stay light, and keep things positive.

You've probably noticed, I've been having a wee wine now and again. I know it's maybe not the answer, but it helps me relax and forget for a while. Who am I kidding, it's constantly on my mind. The cancer. It's everywhere: on TV, adverts, buses, subways, billboards, getting leaflets dropped through our letterboxes, and taxis. I know it's good for people to know and get information; it's just that after I was diagnosed, I started seeing cancer everywhere. Maybe that's just how you notice things after it happens to you. My friend once said to me, once she was pregnant, she saw babies, prams, pregnant ladies everywhere. So maybe it's just how it happens. I've written in my wee book (which I love now) that I'm going to be alright. I feel it sometimes. How's that for positivity? Good on yeh, Carol! You go girl. Love it. Even then, I can read how positive I was, geeing myself up. I've written: I just say to myself, *Get on with it!*

As Billy Ocean—who is a favourite singer of mine, and may I add, sent me a birthday card, sang:

'When the going gets tough, the tough get going.'

Hey Claire, I've written: 'It's a Butterly thing.'

In my wee book, I have also written that I am sitting here thinking about Claire and Laura. Not that I don't often think of them, I do, every single day, but tonight, I'm thinking about how they're coping with this problem of mine.

I have said to them, they can discuss it with their friends if it helps, and get support from them, because it's someone outside the family. Sometimes that works.

Jim did something similar. He went to see Peter, the minister who married Ryan and Kirsty. He is such a lovely man, and Jim chatted with him for over an hour. Jim said talking to Peter helped him. He felt better after that.

I won't get the results of the MRI until the 8th of March, according to my wee book. The appointment on the 1st of March was cancelled, my wee book says, because of the bad weather.

I just hope it's not too bad news. Telling my girls is the worst I have had to do. Fingers crossed all is okay, or as best as it can be.

I'm working tonight, 4-8 shift, to make up for not going in last night. I hope it's a quick shift.

Gartnavel phoned to confirm the appointment, it's scheduled for Thursday the 8th at 10:40 a.m.

Laura is off today; her shop is closed due to the weather. Claire's not at her work either. Neither is Jim, he went out to go but turned back. Nancy's not at work either. Only me! Weather causing havoc everywhere.

Wee Jess was funny in the snow this morning, it practically buried her. She was bopping up and down like a wee rabbit. Also, she is white in colour, so it was hard to see her at times.

My shift wasn't too bad, went in quick, but by God it was freezing! I've written, and that's in the store. At the back was even colder where I have to go and get the new stock. Jim came to meet me to help me over the road, as they were quite icy by this time of night.

I had homemade soup and Angel Delight. I love that dessert, it had been years since I last had it. I went to bed early, around 11:00 p.m., as I was really tired, but as usual, I lay awake for ages. It was beginning to form a pattern. I must have finally fallen asleep around 3 a.m.

I feel it's been a very long week. Still heavy snow on the ground. I took wee Jess out; she was jumping about like a wee rabbit again. Jackie, my supervisor from Nutmeg, asked me if I could go in early, so I am going in at 2 instead of 4. I had a lovely bath and got ready for work. Hope it's a quick shift. I seem to be saying that a lot lately, I noticed.

I got into work. Jackie, my supervisor, said she got an email that delivery was suspended, she only got it 10 minutes before I was due to start. It was absolutely baltic in the Nutmeg cage at the back of the store in Morrisons. Nutmeg has a walk-in cage for all their stock to get wheeled into on pallets. Incidentally, they are really heavily packed and quite a job to push and pull. Nine times out of ten, you are on your own doing this job. Most of my shifts, especially the back shifts, I was always on my own. I didn't mind, really, but it could get lonely sometimes.

As I say, it was always baltic at the back door. The doors were always open for deliveries. I worked four hours, then went for my break, if only to hold onto the cup of tea to heat my hands up!

I finished my shift and Jim met me at the store, get me being all American! We got some shopping, then we came home. I had my homemade lentil soup, and Jim had made a baked potato and tuna. I was hungry, as I hadn't eaten anything since early morning. *Not good for you!* 'Here we go again,' I hear you say.

I had a couple of glasses of wine to relax. I watched *Heat*—Sandra Bullock, one of my very favourite actresses. I love her bone structure, and I think she is very pretty. If I had a pound for every time I have said that to my girls, I would be living in a chateau. 'Château Papillon'—Papillon is French for butterfly. I love it.

Coming away from my dream and back to reality, I enjoyed the movie, then went to bed.

The next morning, not sure if I had a good night's sleep, I didn't write anything about it. I might be called in today if deliveries arrive. Manjeet, a young university student who recently started with us, was on his own and the deliveries were piling up. I told him to call me if he needed help, too much for one person. No phone call, so I just caught up with the washing, etc.

Then Jim and I sat most of the day watching movies, one after the other, binge watch. It was a very lazy day. I have written it down, sounds like it to me. I had a, you've guessed it, a wee glass of wine... or three. It was the weekend. We sat up until 4:00 a.m. I wasn't the least bit tired. I probably will be later on, maybe tomorrow.

I got up at 10:00 a.m. After all, it's Sunday, long lies on Sundays are the norm in our house. I busied myself around the house, you know, the usual bits and pieces. Jim was making steak pie for our dinner later on, love it! It's still snowy outside, though I'm not sure how much longer it will last.

I organised wee Miley's toy box. She needs some older toys; I'll get them tomorrow. It started snowing again. I'm definitely going out tomorrow, even if it's just for some fresh air.

We went to Morrisons, big wow! Today is Monday and it's still slushy and very slidey. I took wee Jessie out. She was walking on the snow rather than the part of the road that had been cleared. Strange wee dog, but we love her. She's *our* strange wee dog.

Jessie didn't do her business. Maybe she sensed something wasn't quite right. You know what they say, dogs can sense things. They say. I don't know... maybe *they*, whoever they are, could be right.

I went to Morrisons, slipping and sliding all the way there. That song *Slip Sliding Away* comes to mind. I got a couple of bags of shopping and came home. I made a roast for later. It smelled delicious, the aroma of the silverside in the oven filled the house.

I'm planning to make haddock with porridge oats later in the week. You can tell I love my food, not so much the cooking! I have written that down in my wee book. For a wee book, it's holding a load of information. And as I am writing this, I am glad, *really* glad, that I have it all to look back on. I would've forgotten half of it otherwise.

Later on, the usual, I relaxed and watched TV. I also do crosswords, may I add, not just a TV fan, and I'm a wee dab hand at knitting: babies' hats, jackets, dresses, and small hats for the premature babies in the maternity units. So, all in all, I try to keep myself busy.

The next morning, I had the usual, breakfast, then got Jess out for her walk. The weather was a bit milder, still slushy, and snow still all around.

I got a letter from Gartnavel Hospital, changing my appointment from 1:30 p.m. to 10:30 a.m. I nearly started crying when I saw the first line of the letter saying 'CANCELLED'. Then I sat down and read it through.

I've waited two weeks for this appointment, to find out what is happening with me and my breast cancer. Have I got it? Do I have it? How bad is it? Can it be sorted? If so, then what is the next step, *if* there is one?

I was reading this letter, but my mind was running riot in my head, as you can imagine, or maybe not. Like I said earlier, with anything that happens in life, you can sympathise, but you never know your real feelings until you're in that position. Until you hear those horrible three words: 'YOU HAVE CANCER.'

I've tried these past few weeks to stay positive, but you can only keep that up for so long. Positivity only lasts as long as the support around you does, like communication between the doctor and surgeon. Even just a little bit of that can work wonders on your mind and your confidence.

I was called into work early today, 2 to 8, instead of my usual 4 to 8 shift. Extra hours, not that I asked for them, but it's better to be at work and keep busy. The delivery for Nutmeg was double the amount because last week's didn't go through due to the bad weather. As I say, better to be there than to mop around the house with Jim pottering about.

The shift went by quickly, as it usually does when you have got extra pallets to do and new stock coming in. I quite liked my wee job. As I have mentioned before, I was on my own most of the time, so I could take my break when I was ready for it.

One more day to go until I get the results. I hope they are good, or as good as they can be.

The shift wasn't too bad, and it went in quite quickly. When I got home, Jim had already made my tea, lovely, it was. You know yourself, it's always more enjoyable when it's been prepared for you.

I relaxed and started reading one of the books I got from the library. I took out five, and one for Jim, his usual: crime, gangster, that type. Big day tomorrow. Fingers crossed. Once again, I'm hoping for good news.

Here we are at last—MRI results day.

Fingers crossed again. Prayers said. God, be kind.

Appointment: Gartnavel, 10:40 a.m. As I remember, the time was changed to an earlier slot.

Jim and I waited for three hours. During that time, I had another scan and another biopsy. They had found another lump, this time on the opposite side of the left breast.

Strangely, I had actually felt the second lump myself a few days earlier and was planning to mention it at the very next appointment. But the consultant brought it up before I even had the chance to speak. The prayers and the strength I tried to hold onto… they felt like they were all for nothing.

When the consultant told us, Jim's face went white as a sheet. He just stared ahead, and I could see his mind was working overtime.

I was just—numb. I felt like I should say something. I tried, but my mouth was dry, and no words came out. Not a sound. I don't know why I couldn't speak. I wanted to, but couldn't.

I just stared into space, looking past the consultant at the beige wall behind him, searching for answers.

The girls spun in my head.

What and how was I going to explain this to them?

Nancy.

Family.

What to do?

My head was going round and round, and I was beginning to get a splitting headache, like a migraine building up.

We left the hospital and got into the car. We drove home in complete silence. We didn't know what to say to each other. This was something we had never dealt with before, and we weren't sure how to begin to decipher this horrific news.

We took our wee dog Jess out for a walk, then went to Wetherspoons for a bite to eat. We were hungry, we hadn't eaten all day. We stayed there until about teatime, just sitting and talking about things. We talked about how far cancer research has come, and how much more they can do for cancer sufferers. There are new treatments, better drugs, and better chances.

They can shrink the tumours, offer drugs that prolong life, radiation, chemotherapy… So we sat there and spoke about all of that sort of stuff. Not a happy subject, but one that has to be approached at some point.

Then we just chatted about every day, ordinary things, as you do. I enjoyed it, though. Especially just trying to talk and understand things together. It felt like good therapy for both of us. I was not trying to analyse it, it just made us feel better.

I always enjoy it when Jim and I go for our wee lunches, but this one was very different.

We came home from Wetherspoons, and by that time, I was feeling very tired. I read some of my book, then went to bed. Usually, I lie awake for ages before I fall asleep. But even after the news I received today, it wasn't long before I was snoring, or so Jim informed me, as he left the room and went into the spare room to try and get some sleep himself.

It had been a very tiring and surreal day.

I called in sick to work today, as I was still sore from the biopsy yesterday at the hospital. I spoke to Jackie, my supervisor, and then called the absence line. He took a note of it.

You know it's actually quite sunny today, I hadn't noticed until now, with the snow finally washed away.

I keep going over and over in my mind what was said yesterday. It's all so surreal. You really do feel like just a number. I hate to think like that, but sometimes it just feels like that.

I know the NHS does their best with the facilities they have, and I truly believe they should receive all the support and funding they need.

Let's hope again that the other lump is not cancer. Maybe it's just a wee cyst. But the consultant said it's likely to be another cancer. And if it is, then everything changes. It'll mean a totally different operation.

Then she said the words: 'You may lose your left breast.'

That was a shock. Up until that moment, I thought I was going to have something like keyhole surgery to remove the tumour, and that I would still have my left breast, scarred but intact.

I'm not sure how I feel about this. I have been writing about it all in my little book—my journey. To say I was shocked is an understatement. Maybe I have just been naïve, or in denial about what might really be in store for me. No one had ever said I might lose my breast. The thought hadn't even crossed my mind.

Then I started to wonder… what would that look like in a swimsuit? In a blouse? A T-shirt? V-neck tops?

I stopped wearing bikinis years ago, but I still like to go swimming on holiday. All this was going on in my head. Will I still be able to feel my breast? I have heard on TV that amputees can still feel their missing limbs or body parts.

I don't want to lose it. But it's not looking good.

I find myself, when I'm having a shower, talking to my right breast. Just trying to explain what is about to happen. People might think I'm going mad, but apparently this is normal. You're supposed to say goodbye to the part of your body you're about to lose. The doctors say it helps with the process.

Colin and Janice, Kirsty's mum and dad, came up that night with Ryan, Kirsty, and their daughter, Miley. They were concerned for Jim and me. The whole family were.

I hated putting this burden on them. But what could I do? Pretend it wasn't happening? Jim and I needed all the support we could get to get through the road ahead.

We had a wee glass of wine, and Jim said to me, 'Try not to drink too much,' as I was getting tipsy rather quickly.

Seriously, who gives a shit? I thought to myself.

I know he means well. But Jesus, if he were the one who'd just been told that kind of news, I'm pretty sure he would reach for a wee half as well. Maybe just to calm himself down a bit. Or... I don't know.

Help him relax a bit. Maybe that's the wrong word, but you get the gist of what I'm trying to say, I hope. As I said earlier, the wee wine helped me relax. Granted, it's not the answer, but no harm was done to anyone. And the banter, as we say in Scotland, flows when there is a wee sherbet had by the company.

Anyway, as Frank Sinatra says, he'll do it his way. That is, me dealing with the cancer. I'm not doing anyone any harm, probably only myself.

I was feeling a wee bit nauseous today. No surprise there, eh? Must have been that wine I keep going on about. I say it relaxes me, and it really does. It takes some stress away.

I just pottered about the house today, as you do, tidying up, etc. Wee Jess and I went for a wee walk, trying to get some fresh air and clear my head a bit. Wee Jess doesn't know what's going on, but they say dogs are very sensitive to what's happening around their wee family. I have a feeling wee Jess knows something is not right. She's very clingy to Jim and me these days.

Claire and Junior came down for a wee visit tonight. Everyone is trying to be upbeat about this bloody thing that's upset our routine and our lives. We are just trying to get on with things as normal. Claire and Junior arrived, and we had a great wee chat about all sorts of stuff. I couldn't discuss what was happening or going to happen to me, as I haven't any news to share yet. But I could see the worried look on their faces. I will let them know as soon as I find out. I never wrote anymore about that visit in my wee book.

The next day was Mother's Day. I woke up at 6:30. 'EGGYBILL'—that's a word my nephews used when they had eaten something dodgy that made them awfully sick. Well, this was the right time for that word, believe me. The bile was involved too. I know it's not a nice thing to talk about, but it happened, so I have to. If it's in my wee book, then it's definitely going in this one. If it weren't for my wee book, I wouldn't have all this information. I may have blocked it from my mind.

I was sick about seven times, and that's no exaggeration. Honestly, see when I was younger and out with the girls from work, I was always sick in the morning. It was always the dreaded bile. It very seldom escaped me or my stomach. I don't think I had the stomach to drink with my friends. I hear you say, 'Maybe I had too much?', no, that wasn't it. Whether I had one or three, I was still sick.

It was 12 o'clock midday before I started to feel any better. I made some chicken noodle soup, that is always my saviour. It's the best thing for a hangover, I kid you not, or even when you're under the weather. (Never understood that statement, 'under the weather', but it was always being said. isn't it?) I always gave that soup to my girls whenever they weren't feeling very well. A wee bed on the couch and a wee bowl of chicken noodle soup made you feel a whole lot better. They still take it to this day, and so does their mother. And our Nancy would put her house on it too. She also loves it.

Jim went to see Peter. Mind Peter, the one who married Ryan and Kirsty? He goes now and then to visit him and have a chat. I'm not sure if it's helping him, but surely it can't do any harm. He's a man of the cloth, as they say, so he should be able to give Jim sound advice, I hope. Peter's wife isn't too well either, Jim told me. Poor man, he has a lot on his plate, as they say. And he still makes time to see Jim. Peter is someone Jim can offload on. Sounds awful, but that's the reality of it.

I received an Amazon parcel. It was a book my Claire had ordered for me. I look forward to reading it. I love reading, it's escapism into the world of the book and helps you forget your own problems for a while.

Laura came to see me after her work. My house has been full of visitors lately. Our Nancy has been making the tea and looking after everyone who comes to the house. She's such a wee diamond. She won't like me calling her 'wee', but she has the biggest heart of anybody I know. If it's possible for her to do something for you, she will. And if not, she'll try her damnedest to get it done.

Wee Nancy, my sister, but a giant in my eyes.

Laura gave me a beautiful bangle with an inscription on it. It reads: *You Are Braver Than You Believe, Stronger Than You Seem, and Smarter Than You Think.*

I will try my best to be all it says on my bangle. What a beautiful gift. I will always keep it with me. It's my most precious gift, as it means so much to me. I was so emotional, I tried not to cry, but my eyes were filling up. As would yours, I imagine, if this were happening to you. It's only natural, we're only human after all.

I don't mean to sound harsh by saying this to you, the reader. I hope it doesn't sound like that. I also received a beautiful pair of earrings. They had a blue stone in them, which is my favourite colour. Just the style I would have picked for myself, honestly. Later, I made a chicken dish. I wrote in my wee book that the dish was rubbish. Must be losing my touch, not sure how that happened! I'm usually not too bad a cook, Jim will vouch for that. He thinks I'm quite a good cook. I'll tell you who is a great cook, my sister-in-law, Claire. Junior's wife. I have never eaten anything she has cooked that I didn't like. Seriously. And I'm not 'sooking in', as we say in Scotland, that means trying to keep in with people. You can ask anyone who has tasted her food. Her kitchen is always busy with her grandkids and their friends, all trooping down for her homemade scran. Anyway, back to my cooking, Gino D'Acampo I am not! I took a Zzz tablet, as I have written in my wee book, still having bother sleeping. Oh, how I love this wee book. I will keep this wee book forever, even after I have all the information from this wee diamond.

I was feeling a wee bit down today, not much, just a wee bit. Maybe it's because I was thinking that yesterday could have been my last Mother's Day. What a horrible thought. But you can't help the thoughts that come into your head, especially when you least expect them.

I don't mean to sound morbid thinking like that, but it's what goes on in my mind. 'Snap out of it', says my wee book, so I'm taking my wee book's advice and going to be as upbeat as I can.

Anyway, I'm going to potter about the house, as I say. I'll try and play a bit of guitar. I'm hopeless at it, my blue guitar, the one Jim got me for Christmas last year. I just can't get my head around the chords. So, I put on YouTube and try to follow the instructions, but I find it hard.

I usually end up just sitting there strumming some nonsense, kidding myself on, pretending it resembles some sort of music. It sounds good, or half-decent, to me. God knows what Jim thinks of it. I can't tell by his face; it looks normal to me.

Oh! He's just turned the volume of the TV up. There's my answer. That says it all.

I put the blue guitar aside and went to make jelly and ice cream. We like jelly and ice cream. It's been a while since I had some, years maybe.

Later on, I did a washing, then an ironing. Anything to keep busy. Laura is going to a gig tonight. Jim is teasing her and taking the mickey, saying he will be there. He told her he would meet her at the venue. She's what you would call panicking, sh****** a brick, to be honest, in case he does actually show up!

She said to him, 'You'll look like a paedo, as there are all young ones there!' Later that night, Jim was texting Laura saying, 'I'm waving to you, Laura. Can you see me? I'm jumping up and down, I have got a pink jumper on!'

It is things like that that get me through this. He is so funny. The banter between those two is priceless. They seem to bounce off each other and get on so well together, which is a Godsend, I think.

Jim also gets on with my older daughter, Claire, it's just different. With Laura, they seem to be on the same page. I would have loved to have seen Laura's face when he sent those texts to her. She wouldn't have put it past him to actually turn up!

David, my nephew, and also my godson, Claire and Junior's youngest son, came up to see me. I'll never forget the look on his face. This was my first time seeing him since I got the bad news, and he was going on holiday the very next day. I hope this doesn't put a damper on his holiday.

Oh! Why do things like this happen? There is never a good time, Is there?

I really appreciate David coming down to see me, especially since he has a small family and works very hard. His time is well taken up with all of that. Love you loads, Godson, as I do all my nephews and nieces.

I have not mentioned my breast cancer for a few pages. It's still on my mind, obviously, 24/7, but I am trying to let the reader know that I am doing my best to live as normal a life as I can, under the circumstances.

I also try not to put too much stress and pressure on my family, so I don't bring the cancer up a lot of the time. Let's be honest, people will get fed up listening to you going all medical and constantly talking about it.

Only if they ask me questions about what's happening will I answer them. Still no word from the hospital as yet.

There is a saying: 'No news is good news.' No point worrying until you have to. There is also another wee saying I heard recently: 'Worrying is the thief of joy.' What a brilliant and true saying. Never a truer word spoken, in my opinion. I love that saying, my wee book loves it too, as I have written it over and over again in its pages.

Not that it stops you from worrying. It is not like a switch, as we all know, you can't just turn it off. If only. It would be half the battle, and there'd be less stress.

Now it's time to get back into the daily routine. The next morning, I took wee Jess out for her usual walk. When I got back in the house, the window cleaner called for his money. As I always say, life goes on.

Wee Jess wanted to go with him, she would go with anybody, I think. She's such a sociable wee dog. As I mentioned earlier, I'm not sure what her wee issues are. They never told us anything when we got her from the rescue.

I got ready to go to the shops. I fancied a wee run in the car to Milngavie for some shopping. I also had a wee rummage in the wee shops in the square there. It's a lovely wee town centre, I like going there, and I enjoy the wee drive in.

I got some shopping, two bags full, may I add, and it cost a blooming fortune, that Milngavie! It's really quite expensive. I was only going in for a few things, as us females always do. But it never works out that way, does it, ladies?

I came home with a few dinners in the bag, so that wasn't too bad. That, to me, was a bonus. Sometimes I'm in the shops, looking at the shelves and saying to myself, 'What am I doing here? What am I looking for?' My mind goes blank. I have no ideas for dinner, no ideas for anything. You're better goof going home when it gets like that, you just end up wasting time and money, seriously.

We buy things we think we might need later on. What's the psychology in that? Two to three days later, they end up in the bin or in a drawer somewhere in the house, never to see the light of day. I bet we all have little knick-knacks and gadgets in a drawer. Example: erasers, novelty pens, odd keys, pins, worn-out nail files, a blob of Blu Tack, elastic, string, etc. And many more trivial things.

We clean out the drawer now and again, but somehow these wee trinkets, as I call them, always make their way back to the drawer. It's weird. Of course, it's 'just in case'.

When I was in Milngavie, I bought a wee box of 'bake your own muffins'. Get me, eh? Mary Berry of Anniesland! This is what happens when you're trying to keep your mind from thinking about your illness. I'm gonna give it a go, hey, it might be fun. They may turn out all right, well, edible, I hope!

I'm no baker, but I once won a baking competition at school for making an Easter cake. I was 12. I was so proud of that wee cake. I made the nest from shredded wheat dipped into chocolate and shaped it to look like a bird's nest. It looked so real and effective. Then I put those little speckled eggs on top, like wee chicks' eggs. Not sure how it tasted, but it looked the part, the teacher said.

I can remember that day as if it were yesterday. Funny that, isn't it? Nothing else significant about that day, just the cake.

Back to baking the muffins, this will probably end up one big sponge cake.

Our Nancy has been so supportive, always asking if I need anything from the shops or need anything done in the house. I get the feeling she doesn't know how to handle everything and keeps herself busy so as not to worry herself sick. I told her it's all going to be fine.

Garry, Nancy's son, is feeling the same. I can see it in his face. I find when I'm in their house, they try not to say the wrong thing in case they upset me. It must be hard for them. I just try and keep the banter going, keep the chat light, and don't mention hospitals, appointments, or anything involved with my diagnosis. What am I saying, I haven't been diagnosed with anything yet.

Our Nancy, as I've said before, has a heart of gold. She would literally take the shoes off her feet and give them to you to walk home in. She'd give you her last, she would. She's a victim of her own kindness, and lots of people take that for weakness. It used to drive me mad, which is outrageous. I get so angry with those people, and to make matters worse, these are people who work with her and know her well.

I love her dearly. She would generally go to the moon and back for you, then go back again to get a star, no kidding. She always sees the good in people. She's still the same to this day. That's just our Nancy.

I can't say how the muffins turned out, as I never wrote down what happened to them in my wee book. Oh well, never mind. Knowing my baking, they would have tasted divine, or just okay.

I just relaxed in the evening and read my book that Claire got me. She also got me the second volume. I love it. Not enough time to read it all at once.

To let you understand: my wee book is where I wrote all about my journey. Once I finished writing in it, I put it in my bedside cabinet and left it there. Then I came across it, and that's when I decided to write this book, about my journey and how I got through it.

My shift today is 4 to 8, so I had the morning to get organised, take Jess out, and watch the usual TV programmes. Not that I stare at the TV all day, it's mostly for background noise. It feels like you're not alone in the house.

I got ready for work. It was okay. There was a woman who knows the family who came up to me and said, 'Carol, I heard your bad news. I'm so sorry. Hope it all goes well for you.' I thanked her and went back to getting on with my shift. I couldn't fully concentrate on my work, as my mind was on tomorrow.

I got lovely texts from friends, family, and work colleagues, loads of good wishes from everyone. Not everyone knew, but family and friends did. I fully appreciated the well wishes.

I'm not sure what Jim was thinking around this time, as he never really spoke about it much. He has his way of dealing with things, in his own way.

Claire and David were on holiday and took time out to send me a lovely text to wish me well. As I said previously, everyone has been brilliant.

And they are there for me at the drop of a hat. I wrote in my wee book, 'You know who you all are,' and I cannot thank you all enough.

The Butterlys are something else, love you, *se*. My Claire has been a tower of strength for me. She's far away from me, well, not really, she lives and works in Edinburgh, but it feels like a long way sometimes. She comes through to Glasgow, work permitting, and as often as she can. She brings her wee dog with her. She has a corgi, a beautiful little dog. Claire got her when she was a puppy. She was just like a wee cuddly teddy bear. She is one of the family now, another addition to the Butterlys. Her name is Arya.

Laura has been so strong. She has been popping in to see me every chance she gets, and she really cheers me up with her wicked sense of humour. She's brill. Of course she is, she is mine! Both of my girls are brilliant. They both have a great attitude to life, and I learn a lot from both of them. They are coping so well with this. I never imagined how this would play out, but you two (I'm talking to my daughters now), if I can say this to you: I am so, so proud of you both, then, now, and always.

'The Three Amigos', we used to call ourselves. We would do that daft wee dance they did, then shout 'HEY!' at the end of the song. What were we like, eh?

Today is the biggie, getting the results of the biopsy for the other lump on the same breast, but on the opposite side. Hopefully... but I have a feeling it's not going to be good news.

Travelling to the hospital was tense, to say the least. Hardly a word was spoken. I just wanted to get there and get it over with. It was what I thought and what I was dreading. Mr Malloy, the consultant, said to me that because both growths were on the same breast and on opposite sides, the breast had to be removed.

My intake of breath was so loud I shocked myself. I tried to keep it together. I didn't look at anyone in the room, I just stared straight ahead. Mr Malloy spoke very soft and gentle, but I wasn't taking in any of the words he was saying. I just saw his lips move. But the words "removal of breast" were repeating themselves over and over again in my head.

I gave myself a shake after what felt like ages, because I had to listen and take in all the information he was giving me. It was important. He was asking me questions too, but he said not to answer them now. He said he was making another appointment to see me very soon and that I should write all my questions down and bring them with me next time.

He took the time to let me consume all this information. What a lovely, decent, and very considerate young man, well, he was about mid-40s. That's young to me!

Then that was it. Mr Malloy said he would send in the breast nurse to see me, told me to take care and try not to worry, and then he was gone.

Well, that's the first thing you do when he leaves the room, isn't it? Worry.

I went to leave the room, not sure what I was thinking, when the breast specialist nurse came in. She was very nice. Her name was Anne, and she started to explain my options.

My one option was to bail out, but I never had that option.

Now these nurses must hear this kind of news every day, more than once a day, I imagine. I know it's hard to believe, but these clinics are full nearly every day. I know because I saw it for myself. I was shocked at how busy the clinics were.

Anne gave me a DVD and some leaflets to take home. She said I'd probably have to watch the DVD a few times to take in all the information. She also said she would make an appointment for me to see a plastic surgeon.

WHAT!

I've written this in my booky in large letters: 'to discuss what operation would suit me and if my tissue was suitable.'

Whit?! I'm no getting measured up for a suit! What's happening here?

I wrote that down in my wee treasure book.

I took the information Anne had given me and put it in my bag. We left the room and made our way to the car. I have to go home and speak to my girls about all of this.

The first thing I have to do is read these leaflets and watch the DVD, and digest as much of this as I can.

Mr Malloy said the operation, a mastectomy and reconstruction, would take around eight hours in theatre.

I can't understand why they call it *theatre*. It's hardly entertaining, is it? You can't watch anything, you're out for the count! You miss all the best bits.

I wrote that down as a bit of banter: 'I'll be missing my bits, or, more precisely, my "lefty" boob. That's what I'm calling it now.'

You know when I was in the shower, as I said earlier, I spoke to my right breast. Might sound crazy, but this thing does crazy things to you and your mind.

I said to it, let's call it "Righty", 'You are going to miss your Lefty booby buddy. But it's not my fault. It's what's called life. You're probably going to be lonely… but hey, you're still here. It could have been worse; you might have been taken too.'

Sounds normal talking like that, don't you think?

I don't know if that's part of what happens when you're going down this road. Nobody has said anything to me to suggest it isn't normal.

So, onwards and upwards, until I'm told different.

I won't tell anyone if you don't.

I have a lot to think about and discuss. Jim is anxious for us to go away for a wee break before all this takes place. I can understand his idea, but it's not first on my list at the minute.

Right now, I'm not sure he is coping very well. As I say, he doesn't talk about it, so how are you supposed to know how he's really feeling.

If I ask him, he just says, 'I'll cope with it.'

I spoke to Junior on the phone. He sounded very sad. I said, 'I'll be okay, Junior,' and I've written that, it will.

I had weird dreams last night. I tossed and turned the whole night. I was still awake when the light broke through the curtains, getting brighter and brighter. All this stuff was churning in my mind about the operation.

I have a shift at work today, 4 to 8, the usual. I find it hard when I'm in work to concentrate on people and work stuff: orders, palettes, deliveries, and the whole shebang. Then there are customers complaining about sizes, colours, shades, wrong items. I like dealing with customers and helping them get what they need. I'm always helpful and polite, and I do what I can to solve their problems.

I was the same when I worked in Marks & Spencer many years ago. But you get the odd customer who really takes the biscuit and complains just for the fun of it, to stand by and watch you getting into trouble with your supervisor. It's happened to me before. To them, it's a life-or-death situation if they don't get what they want. Oh, please, get a life!

I'm going to relax just now before I get ready for my shift. You're probably saying to yourself, 'Why is she bothering with her shift?' Well, there is nothing else much to do while I wait for my next appointment to come through the letterbox. So, I might as well keep mobile and do something productive, or I would just curl up in bed. That won't be much use to me. I'd end up all stiff, sitting so long in the one position.

I say that to myself to keep going: BE POSITIVE! It is written in big letters more than once in my book. Sounds like I'm gambling, and I have got a wee wager going with myself. Yeh, maybe unconsciously, I have? Hope I win.

Going back to the operation, the reconstruction part of it, Mr Malloy says they take skin and muscle from your stomach and make a boob from it. Amazing what they can do, eh? So, you are also getting a tummy tuck into the bargain.

When I said this to Claire and Laura, they said, 'Mum, you always wanted to try and get rid of your tummy. Maybe not this way, granted.'

We all laughed. It's true, ever since I had my two girls, I have tried on numerous occasions to lose it.

Mr Malloy said there would be a scar from hip to hip, that's only if the skin and tissue are a match. I hope they are. The other way they can do it is to take a muscle and skin from your back and bring it over your shoulder towards where your boob was. There's a medical name for it, but at the minute, I can't remember. Sounds horrendous to me!

Anyway, here's hoping that all goes well and that I will be suitable. I think I would rather go for the boob reconstruction and tummy operation all together, the right-hour operation.

I had to get ready for my shift. Jackie, my supervisor, texted me. I should have been in at 2 to 6. This was 2:45 at the time, and I was still in the house! Thinking about the operation made me lose track of time. Just as well I live just over the road from Nutmeg, so it wouldn't take me long to get over there.

I quickly got ready and went to work. I finished at 7:00 p.m., came home, and made some homemade lentil soup. It's one of my favourites. It was lovely, if I say so myself.

I called Nancy and had a wee gab with her. She's coming over tomorrow around 3:00 p.m., probably coming to have some of my lovely lentil soup. I will give her some to take home so she won't have to cook later.

When she gets home, I watched TV and had a wee, and I mean a *wee,* glass of red wine, then went to bed around 1:30 a.m.

Today, I'm taking wee Jess to get her nails clipped. They are so sharp, especially what's called her dew claws, the smaller ones further up her paws. She's been a wee godsend, really. Great company for me.

I said earlier, she was a wee rescue dog. We are working on getting her over the wee issues she has. She is such a wee cutie at times. Other times, not so much, but hey! We brought her into our family, so we have to give her a chance. She is scared of the least wee noise. We were never told what happened to her in her early years. She was about 18 months when we got her.

I'm going to need to get my car looked at.

I have a black Peugeot, which I love, and I love driving it. I noticed the exhaust is hanging down a bit, so that's not so good. Just like *mwah* these days.

That's another thing: after the operation, I won't be able to drive, argh, for a while. I never gave that a thought. Jim will have to be my chauffeur. Unpaid, of course. Not sure if he'll like being at my beck and call. Sounds okay to me, ha ha! I'll get him a wee lunch in Wetherspoons; he'll like that. I think that's a good deal for him.

I took my wee car to the garage in Bearsden. Jim told me about the garage there, they are pretty reasonable, he said.

Nancy came to mine for dinner. Special fish supper, oh, what a treat that is! I love them. Don't get them that often, so it *is* a treat when we do. It doesn't get better than that.

She took wee Jess home with her to give me a wee break. A long lie in the morning, no need to take wee Jess out for the toilet. Anyway, she will be good company for Nancy.

Nancy had two dogs of her own over the years, but they're gone now. Trudy, a collie cross, she was like a Lassie dog. She was so beautiful. Chester, her other dog, was a lurcher, part mongrel, I think. They were both great dogs.

My daughter Claire grew up with Trudy, and Claire loved that dog.

I watched TV, then I had a glass of Hardy's, as you do. Lovely, no worries. I'm keeping tabs on my intake.

Jim made me a lovely breakfast and brought it into the bedroom. Yeah, breakfast in bed, what a treat! It was lovely. Then I got dressed, and we went to IKEA. We got some bits and bobs that we needed. You can't go into that shop and not come out with something, either something you need or something you didn't need. It never fails. You buy it because you know you'll need it *sometime*.

We came out with plants, a grill pan, a meat tenderizer, wine glasses, etc. I'm sure we could have done without these, but there you are. It happens.

Jim and I are nitpicking at the moment. You get days like that. I think everyone does, now and again, especially with what's on our minds. We are trying to keep things as normal as we can, but it can be hard at times. I need to stop going on about it and just get on with it. Positivity!

I'm sorry if I'm repeating myself sometimes, but as I am writing, things just pop into my head.

Anything I say today, Jim has an answer for, and a better one than I have. No kidding, it's doing my head in.

And he is getting on my fekking nerves. He's not always right, but he doesn't see that. He thinks he is most of the time. It's so annoying. He says he can't say anything right these days, well, he should think before he speaks and consider what's going on around him. He can be so critical at times. He's been like that before, but he's getting worse with age. Now that he's getting older, he won't agree with you, he'll say everyone else is wrong. What a guy!

He says we're all so sensitive these days. I beg to differ. Well, maybe he should throw some of that sensitivity my way, because he's not very sympathetic. I'm not looking for "poor me" or to be wrapped up in cotton wool. I have always been independent in my life. But a wee bit of caring can go a long way.

I have noticed a change in Jim during this cancer journey. He'd rather deny it is there. He's got to remind himself: *I* am going through this, not him. Someone once said to me, 'I know Jim is going through things that he has never experienced before, but remember, Jim, I'm talking to *you* now, it's happening to *me*.'

I've been really trying hard not to make this out like a big deal. Half the time, I don't even mention anything to do with cancer, even if it appears on the TV. If an advert comes on, he will say, 'Why do they have to put that cancer advert on?' It's getting to him now, and he's lost. He doesn't know what to say or how to deal with it. And I can't help him.

He should go and speak to someone, but I know he won't. He said he'll cope *his* way.

This cancer doesn't just target the person who has the unfortunate roll of the dice. It's like a pebble tossed into a pool of water. The rings get larger and larger and start to spread out to all your loved ones and family and all the links connected to you.

The reason I'm telling you how Jim dealt with it, or didn't, is to let you know how it can affect other people: partners, etc., and how they can't deal with it.

You just can't wade into the water and stop it. It's too strong, and it continues to spread. You just have to control it and not let it get over your head. That's what I've written down, and that's my thought.

Maybe we *shouldn't* be so sensitive these days. But what's the alternative? Turn a blind eye?

Pretend things aren't happening? I'm not sure that's the proper way to deal with it.

Anyway, I'm no Socrates. He believed that no one does wrong voluntarily. Well, I would hope not. Hey, my history stood me in good stead, don't you think? My wee book seems to think so.

I called in sick the next day. I was due a long shift, 12 to 8. I couldn't handle that. I explained to Jackie that I couldn't do a long shift like that. I wasn't prepared for it. I was afraid a customer might ask me for something, and I would just tell them where to go. My mind wasn't on my work.

As the time was getting closer to the operation, my nerves were getting more shredded, and I wasn't interested in my work anymore.

Incidentally, I haven't told you, all through this journey so far, I haven't cried yet. Not at the clinic, not in the car on my own, not in the house, nowhere. I can't explain why, and I don't understand why I haven't. Even to this day. I'm not sure why, as I *do* have tears. Maybe it's because if I don't cry, then it's not real. It's not happening. Even at the time I was told, it felt like it was happening to someone else and not me. It's like I'm on the outside watching this other person, not me. I really distanced myself from it. I never made it personal at the beginning. I had an appointment at the garage to get my wee car sorted.

I hoped it would not be too expensive. I need my wee car to get out and about, otherwise I'd be stuck in the house. It gives you freedom. You don't have to rely on anyone. You just get in and drive, to wherever and whenever you want to go.

The car was sorted, and the price was pretty reasonable. Was I glad? You bet I was.

I had an appointment at the doctor's at 2:30 p.m. Usual morning, took Jess out for her walk and her wee toilet break. I came back and made myself a lovely wee fry-up brekkie: egg, potato scone, bacon, and mushrooms. Good to myself, eh? Why not. It reminds me of the time I was on holiday in Greece, and the guy behind the bar, his name was Mickey, he always wore a black T-shirt with the words "Why Not" in big white letters. And he would always say, 'Another one?' and you would look at him, and he would stick his chest out and say, 'Why Not?' It worked every time. The customers would have another drink, and then some. He was good fun.

Anyway, back at the ranch, as they say. I had a wee chat with Dr Rousse about tomorrow. She was great to speak to.

The receptionist told me later that Dr Rousse had already been through the breast cancer procedure. The receptionist probably shouldn't have told me about the doctor's condition, but I think she thought it would help me to know that she was going through the same diagnosis as myself.

The receptionist aided any time I needed to speak to Dr Rousse; she would put me straight through to her if possible. I thanked her for that, it was good to know. I got a hair dye, going to do my hair tonight. Nothing drastic, just a bit lighter to hide the grey.

I guess there's a lot to take in tomorrow, so I'd best get as good a sleep as I possibly can. I'm planning on going to bed early tonight. Nancy and Claire, my sister-in-law, are coming with me to the hospital to give Jim a wee break. He's actually working. I'm going to give the girls a call and hear how they are coping.

I'm sitting here with the hair dye on, hoping it turns out alright. I've done this loads of times, but you never know. Jim says I look a picture, bet I do! A horror picture! Hair all coiled up on top of my head, with dye running down the side of your face. Like Engelbert Humperdinck. Big sideburns, remember them? If you're old enough, you will, they were massive!

At least when I go to the hospital tomorrow, my hair will be fine, even if I'm not.

I had an appointment to see the plastic surgeon today at 2:15 p.m., Clinic 3. As I said, Nancy and Claire came with me. We were sitting in the clinic when they called my name, and we went into the surgeon's room. We were all apprehensive, as you can imagine. All our faces were grey, even though we had a bit of makeup on. My hair was the only brightness in the room.

Mr Malloy is very nice, as I said earlier, and has one of those voices you could listen to for ages. Very calming. He introduced himself to my family, and then proceeded to ask me what I wanted to do, have the breast removed and reconstruction all at the same time (the eight-hour operation). He needed to know because they need all the surgeons, plastic surgeons, anaesthetists, etc., to be in the same room at the same time. A lot of organising goes into this operation. They need 8 to 12 surgeons, half working on your breast and the other half on your stomach.

That's one option. The other one is an implant. I needed to decide which one is right for me. There's also the flap option I wrote about earlier, pulling a muscle over from your shoulder to over your breast area.

Now, I haven't told you that I watched the DVD a few times before this appointment. The breast nurse, Ann, told me the DVD was very old and that they had moved on a bit since then with better equipment and so on. To say it was a shock to watch it was an understatement. I watched it on my own, of course. I also read up on the leaflets I was given.

So, I had made my decision. I wanted this cancer taken from me as soon as possible. Then, later, I would get my reconstruction. I just wanted this disease out of my body. If it meant losing a breast to do that, then it had to be done. It made me feel dirty to have this in my body, it might sound mad, but that's how I felt.

Ann, the breast nurse, was standing at the table next to Mr Malloy. I noticed she was bouncing on her heels for some reason, anxious to say something. I said to Mr Malloy that I wasn't in favour of the implant or the flap option. So I said to him that I would have the mastectomy. Anne jumped right in and said, 'Carol, I have a date for you.'

I looked at her and said, 'When?'

And she said, 'Monday.'

I was taken aback, it was Friday. Monday was only two days away. I said to her, 'Monday? Monday!?'

I was pretty shocked at how quick this was moving.

Dr Rousse had said to me, 'Don't be surprised or alarmed at how quickly things will start moving.'

I looked over at Nancy and Claire, their face and their eyes were a picture. But we all held it together. Of course we did. We're a strong family, a very strong family, and we're here for each other.

So, all was arranged. I will come to the hospital to be admitted at 7:00 a.m., have the mastectomy, and maybe be home around three days later. I'm glad it's quite soon, it saves all that waiting around and worrying.

So here's to tomorrow, and I hope it's a successful day. I am very nervous and keep hoping, as Bob Marley would say, 'Every little thing's gonna be alright. Don't worry.'

Dr Rousse called me, everyone has been, as I said, very supportive. Junior is coming to see me later this afternoon. He is going to give me some guitar books and some tips. We'll have a wee chat and a good laugh. I'll enjoy his company. He'll play the guitar and sing some songs. A wee karaoke for ourselves.

Sorry, I'm a day ahead! Junior's visit is tomorrow. I have already written it in my bookie. What am I like?

Hopefully, my lymph nodes aren't affected by the cancer and they don't have to be removed.

I called Jackie to let her know what was happening, and that I won't be in at work for a while. I also called Kim, my line manager. You have got to let them know what's going on with you. They were both nice and understanding. Kim said my health comes first and wished me well.

I called Dr Rousse, but the line was engaged. I called the receptionist to say I couldn't get through, and she said she would help me get in touch with her if needed. She must have done just that, as Dr Rousse returned my call. She made me feel at ease and gave me a cover note for my work.

I'm going for my pre-operation tomorrow at 11:30 a.m. I hope all is well and it's full steam ahead for the mastectomy. Nancy and I are meeting up for a wee lunch after the appointment. Laura is going to try and join us too, and we can all go for lunch together.

Claire, my daughter, is going to her school friend Ainsley's wedding this weekend. It's being held in Cameron House, what a beautiful place to have your wedding! I've been there before, to my nephew's wedding. What a backdrop for photographs. I've known Ainsley since she and Claire went to Notre Dame Secondary School together.

Claire will come to see me on Monday, which is great. I can't wait to see her and give her a big hug. Laura's birthday will be while I'm in hospital, but no problem, Laura, I've written that we'll celebrate when I'm up and about. Hopefully, there's that word again, well, if you don't have hope, what is there to cling to?

She is going to be 28. Not sure where all the years have gone? It's flown by so quickly. Gosh! I remember when I was 28, I was already a mother to a one-year-old. I had Clairebear (that was her wee nickname). She also had a Care Bear; they were all the rage at the time. All the kids had them. So many different ones in different colours. Bedtime Bear was Claire's favourite; it had a large moon on its tummy. She also had a smaller one called 'Care Bear'. It was pink. She loved them both.

Tonight, I'm going to see Yvonne and co., she is Jim's daughter, and Mark, her husband. Then we're going on to see Ryan and Kirsty, and wee Miley. Janice too, she is Kirsty's mum, and Colin, her dad. They have all been there for me. Colin and Janice even came to see me at Kirsty's house before I went in for my operation.

Today I'm going to Gartnavel for my pre-operation. I can't wait to get this over with and get rid of this disease. I'll have an ECG, blood test, chest X-ray, and all the other tests that need to be done to prep for the operation.

I'm now all prepped for the operation on Monday. I went to Braehead with Nancy and Laura to get my support bras for after the operation. Laura got herself a pair of Harry Potter PJs. Before that, we had a bite to eat in Wetherspoons. When I got home, Nancy took Jess up the road to her house until after my operation. She might even keep her a bit longer to let me recuperate, and I think she will.

Claire is coming back through from Edinburgh. I'm really looking forward to seeing her, and Arya too. She's staying with me for a few weeks. Right now, I'm just watching TV and writing in my wee book, trying to unwind after today. I'm so tired, oh! I just want to get this over with.

Today we are going to Edinburgh for the *War Horse* concert. I've been wanting to see this for a while now. Jim got us tickets ages ago. We're leaving around 2:00 p.m. Nancy's got Jess, so she will be fine.

We got the bus into town, then the bus to Edinburgh. We arrived at our wee flat for our overnight stay. It was lovely, located in Newington, a 15-minute walk from Princess Street. We got all settled and started to get ready for our evening at the theatre.

Then you will never believe this, the tickets were for another night! Not the date we thought. We were a month too early, ha ha! What are we like? A pair of numpties. Well, not really me, Jim is. He arranged it all. You couldn't make it up, could you?

The tickets were actually dated for some time in May, not March. I'm not sure how that happened. But with everything that's been going on, I'm not surprised. A wee bit of senility on Jim's part, I'm blaming him. It's easier to!

But we were in Edinburgh, so we made the most of it. After all, it was still a wee break away. We went for a meal and did a mini pub crawl. Then we walked to the venue for a dummy run, as you do. We stood outside the theatre and looked at the large poster advertising *The War Horse*. So, at least we now know how to get there on the actual night we do go.

We still enjoyed ourselves on that wee break. Jim and I always do on our wee jaunts out and about. The worst part was that it was Kirsty's birthday that weekend, and we were invited to the party. Of course, we couldn't go, because we thought we had the theatre. What a right pair of idiots we are. So, we missed out on a really good night at Kirsty and Ryan's.

If we had got the bus back to Glasgow that night, we wouldn't have arrived at Kirsty's until very late into the night.

We were still in Edinburgh and went for breakfast, then a walk around the city, through the market, the shops, and tried some of the foods from the wee market stalls.

I still keep thinking of this operation, or say it for what it is. My wee bookie says: *Mastectomy*. It feels it's happening to someone else. I still feel that in me, even after all the appointments, hospital visits, and all the talk about what's taking place. The doctors and nurses... Anyway, I'm going on a bit, sorry.

I enjoyed my break away, but wherever you go, it's always nice to get back home, don't you think? An old cliché, but so, so true on many levels.

One more day before the big day, as they say. Who *are* 'they'? I would like to meet them. 'They', there's that word again, have a lot to say for themselves, don't you think, reader?

We got the bus back to Glasgow, got home, and I packed my wee bag for the hospital. My dressing gown, Jim bought me a new one in Edinburgh. My post-operation bras from M&S, which, incidentally, you get £5.00 off every bra you buy. Not bad, eh? A wee bargain.

We watched a bit of TV that night. We were both very quiet. Didn't say much to each other. What would you expect to say? 'How are you feeling?' Silly question. It's obvious how you're feeling.

Jim and I were both just wanting this over with. It was a very long night for both of us, and for the rest of the family too, I imagine. We were all in this together. I received lots of texts and well wishes on the phone, with everyone asking to send word as soon as we heard anything. I said I would text when I woke up from the operation to let them know how it all went.

I went to bed knowing I wouldn't get much sleep. I watched the clock, until eventually, it came to 6:30 a.m.

Today is here at last. I wrote that in my wee book in big, giant letters.

I barely slept, as was to be expected, I suppose. Neither did Jim. He is still very, very quiet. That's also to be expected.

Not sure what to say to each other. Scared in case we say the wrong thing and we get upset.

Jim put a joint of beef in the slow cooker last night, and the smell was all over the house. Something nice and homely to wake up to, a roast beef dinner. I was fasting, so I couldn't have any. How cruel to cook that when I couldn't eat.

I could see Jim nicking bits here and there. I was salivating. He thought I didn't see him. I said, 'So cruel!' I would have done the same if it were me. Jim put two slices between twice slice of bread and salted it. It looked heavenly to me, and it smelt even better, the best.

We packed the bags, ready to go. Sounds like a song: 'I've packed my bags, I'm ready to go,' only I'm not going on a jet plane.

We arrived at the hospital at 7:00 a.m., Nancy, Jim, and me. It was very quiet at the hospital. Admissions weren't even open. They opened just after 7:00 a.m. The receptionist took all my details, then everything happened so fast after that.

They took me into a room and prepped me for theatre. I had my gown on. Jewellery was taken from me. Nancy and Jim were allowed in to say their goodbyes. I felt for them, the worry on their faces.

They both left.

Just as I was being wheeled to the theatre, there was a lady lying on the other trolley bed in the same room as me. She wished me well, and I wished her well too. What an inspiration she was to become for me. I will tell you more about this incredible lady further along the way of this journey. Her name is Sheila.

The anaesthetist came into the room, put the mask over my face, and told me to take two deep breaths. I did. Then I heard myself saying, 'It's not working! It's not working!' Then, I don't remember anything else.

I must have passed out.

The next thing I remember, I was being brought around from the surgery. The nurse was calling my name and telling me to wake up. I opened my eyes. I couldn't really see clearly at first, then my vision became clearer. I looked up, and the woman beside the bed I was on was Pauline. She is a woman I used to work with at Gartnavel. We both started on the same day and became workmates. Pauline later moved on to another department, she is a theatre orderly now.

I was very surprised to see her. Of course, I was still under the anaesthetic and probably babbling by that time.

I was taken to a ward, then I fell asleep off and on throughout the morning. I'm not sure when I got back to the ward. When I woke up, the lady who had been on the trolley bed next to me when I was taken to theatre was brought into the ward. She was placed in the bed to the left of mine, near the window. My bed was at the entrance to the ward. I had seen this lady every time I went to the clinic.

I actually said to Jim on one of our many visits, 'There's that lady again.' I nicknamed her *Frenchie* because she reminded me of Coco Chanel. She had that French look about her, very chic and stylish.

Well, was I glad she was in the bed next to me. We clicked straight away. The moment we started talking, I found out we were on the same journey. She was 82 years old, and I kid you not, so upbeat, very interesting to listen to, and one brave lady.

We were comparing our experiencing of the operation. We both had drains in from the breast to drain any fluid. It was not painful having the drain in, but the slightest movement tugged on your breast, or rather, on the wound where your breast had been. Especially when you had to go to the toilet, what a palaver! You were in there for ages, but you really had to take it slow. *Real* slow.

I tried a peek down my gown to see how it looked. I don't know what I was expecting, because I was all bandaged up. So, all I saw was the tube coming out the side. Me, I like to look at a wound and see what it looks like. Weird! I know.

We were given painkillers. I noticed Sheila rejected them and said she was okay. I was in awe of her. No painkillers? Brave lady indeed. Then she told me, as we got talking, that she was taking some herbal medicine, and it worked for her. Good on her.

I said to her, 'Here's me praising you for being so brave,' and she just laughed. We were a real tonic for each other. She's really a lovely, genuine person. I've never met anybody like her. She said I nearly burst her stitches with all the laughing we were doing. She also had a wicked sense of humour. I liked her a lot—this *Frenchie*.

It's Laura's birthday today. I sent her a birthday text. Not the best birthday, with me in hospital, but we had to make the best of it. I texted the family to let them know the operation was over and I was fine. Sore, uncomfortable, and in pain, but okay. It's a small price to pay.

They were texting back saying they were glad it was over and that it had all gone okay. Laura is coming up later to visit me. So are Jim, Nancy, Claire, and Junior. I'm looking forward to seeing them.

I felt very tender, well, it *was* early days, I know. But I was still feeling like this was happening to someone else and not me. I feel like I'm walking this person through it, making sure *she is* okay. Not sure why I feel like this. Maybe it's denial, whatever It is, I don't know.

It was great to see Claire, Junior, Nancy, and Laura. They were surprised I was sitting up in bed and talking away, quite the thing. I'm having plenty of pain relief, I need it.

Sheila and I have been given exercises to do. For instance, standing against the wall and putting your arm up as if you're trying to reach something. I'll tell you, it was quite painful. I sound like a right moany person, but I'm not. I *can* take pain.

We had to do this exercise three times a day, to stop the upper arm from stiffening. The nurse says it will get easier the more we do them. As I was doing them, they weren't getting any easier!

The drain in my left boob, or what *was* my left boob, kept getting in the way, as you can imagine. I have to keep it in until Wednesday, two days away. The nurse said it will be taken out before I go home. I can't wait for them to take it out, and to go home.

Don't get me wrong, the staff have been brilliant. They have their work cut out, always very busy. I haven't slept much. The nurse says I have to sleep so I can heal.

Been eating my meals okay. As my girls would say to me, 'Mum, we know you're not well when you can't eat.' They're so right. So as long as I'm eating my food, then I'm okay.

I keep looking and feeling at my left side, still can't believe this is happening to me. The food was actually not too bad in the hospital.

Sheila and I are getting on like a house on fire. We click, as I said earlier. You do that with some people, don't you? I said to Sheila that I'm glad she was in hospital with me, not that I want her to be ill, no, not that way. God forbid. I told her I called her Coco Chanel because she carries herself so regally and she's so serene, I thought. She just laughed.

She told me about her family and her children. She lost a daughter just before Christmas, then this happened to her. She didn't tell any of her family about her mastectomy, just her husband, Robin.

I call her my bosom buddy. We sign off like that on emails to each other.

Today we were told we might get to go home, but our drains are still in. I don't want to go home with this in, and neither does Sheila. We agreed to say we had no one at home to look after us so that we could stay another day. I didn't really feel well enough to go home. At least if something went wrong with the drain, we were in the right place to get it sorted. If I was at home with the drain and something went wrong, I know I would panic. And mistakes could happen when you're in a state of panic.

Last checks for drains, then we got fitted for our new prosthesis boob and our new bra.

The next morning, I was called into a room with the lady that fits your prosthesis. She had some bother with mine, trying to get the proper size. See, they ask your breast measurement before your operation so they can have the prosthesis ready for you. After a good bit of shuggling and manoeuvring this rubbery, heavy, small-football-looking thing, she eventually got it into the bra. Mind that I'm still feeling very tender at this early stage. It felt very tight, as if the top half of my body was in a vice, I kid you not. I personally wasn't sure it was the right size.

I walked into our ward, and Sheila whistled, then she shouted, 'Wheet woo! Hey there, Marilyn Monroe!' I started to sing "Happy Birthday" to Sheila in that soft, sultry way that Marilyn Monroe sang to President Kennedy on his birthday. Well, maybe I didn't sing it the same way she did, or anything like it, but Sheila said it was good.

We sat chatting until teatime, then we were given the good-to-go. Sheila gave me her email address, and I gave her mine so we can keep in touch with each other. We were bosom buddies now and forever.

I called Jim, and he came to collect me. Oh, by the way, our drains got removed earlier that day. It was very cold when we left the hospital. I felt very fragile, as if someone knocked into me, I would fall down. Seriously. Honestly, that's exactly how I felt, and very vulnerable, especially after being in the cocoon of the hospital.

I got home and went straight to my bed. I think I slept most of the afternoon, dozing off and on, with the help of my painkillers. They are quite strong, and thank goodness they are.

Claire and Laura came into the bedroom and sat on the floor. I said to them to sit on the end of the bed, but they said no. I think they were scared in case they hurt me, wee souls. We chatted for hours. I thoroughly enjoyed our chat. We had a laugh also, with their sense of humour, I wasn't surprised.

I could also see the anguish in their faces. I was trying to reassure them that all was okay. I wished I could take their fear away, but of course, I couldn't.

Laura left around 10:30 p.m. She didn't have much of a birthday, up and down to hospital, poor soul. I will make it up to her when I'm feeling a lot better. I said this to her, and she said, 'Mum, plenty time to have my birthday later.'

Laura has to go home in her wee scooter. I don't like her leaving so late at night, especially on her scooter. I asked her to text me when she got home.

Claire and I continued our gab. Claire is staying with me. I love having her here. It's a chance for us to catch up on our news. I felt she was so far away. It's not really, only Edinburgh. A train ride away, and not that long a journey. But to be far away when all this is going on, God love those girls. They have been so strong for me. I'm going to make sure they are okay.

What can I say? It still feels like it's happening to someone else, as I said earlier, and not me. Not sure if this feeling is normal or not. Nobody has said anything about it.

Arya is here with Claire, she's no bother. Jess is at Auntie Nancy's house. I'm missing her, mind you. But the two together don't get on, as wee Jess is too young and wants to play all the time, and Arya is older, and she can't be bothered half the time. They can be a handful together.

I am writing this on Easter Sunday, it says here in my wee book. I didn't have the energy earlier. I'm trying to recall what I did, as the pain is quite sore when I move. It's early days, as they tell me. The scar is very raw at this stage.

I asked Nancy to come into the bathroom to wash my hair, as I can't reach up to my shoulder, never mind my head. She said the scar looks fine. But her face when she saw it, it looked shocked. The scar is from under my arm to the middle of my chest. Anyhow, what an ordeal that was, trying to get in and out of the bath. It took all the energy from me. I was totally shattered after that, went straight back into my bed for a rest.

I just lay in my bed, and Nancy was making me a bite to eat and a cuppa tea, it was lovely. Then I dozed off for a few hours.

I got loads of texts from the family and friends; I really appreciate them all. I couldn't ask for better family and friends. They're all ace.

Jim sometimes doesn't realise when he says something without thinking, it could offend people. He's trying his best, I know, but it doesn't help the situation. As I said earlier, he's not sure how to cope. Neither do I. But you don't talk people down when they're trying their best to help. I'm just going along day by day.

We still haven't spoken about my condition, let's call it that. We're skipping around it at the minute. One thing at a time, I think.

He's always on the defensive. Doesn't he know I'm on his side?

Anyway, it's lots of humour I need just now, cheery, positive people. Jim is lacking in that department right now. Big time.

I mean, he'll say something like, 'Don't you think the visitors are taking too much out of you?' or 'I think we should tell them you're too tired.'

'No,' I said. 'I love having them. When I'm tired, I'll let them know.'

God knows I'm glad to be here.

Claire and Laura text me constantly, and what a sense of humour they both have, It's a tonic for me. Thank goodness they do. I have written it down in my wee bookie; I would never have remembered all this in a million years.

It's good Friday today. I slept most of the time. Jim went to see Peter; I think he is still helping him. Well, I hope he is. Jim doesn't discuss what they talk about. That's fine, I don't mind. I hope Peter can get what's bothering him out of his system.

I missed filling this page in. I'm trying to remember what I did, maybe I was just too tired. It wasn't Jim and I's usual Friday night. We normally have a wee glass or two of something and watch old movies or old music videos after we have finished our work for the week. But I can't take any alcohol while I'm on these heavy painkillers.

Jim had a few wee Drambuies, he loves that. It's so smooth and warms you all over, it's like velvet liquid. I suggest you try one, you won't be disappointed, I can assure you. I've written in my wee book that I have a liking for a wee Drambuie.

I've been texting so much lately, never texted so much before, especially not in the last couple of months. Gosh, what a couple of dark months it has been. One day you're working away, and the next, BANG!

It just knocks you sideways. It's true what they say: just as well you don't know what's around the corner, you wouldn't cope if you did. Well, I don't think so. So all that's left is to pick myself up, as the song says, dust myself down, and start all over again, with a little help from my friends. (Another wee song, that's plagiarism for you.)

Same with today—I am just worn out. This page was blank for a while.

I went for a bath. Not the first time I have had one, but when I looked in the mirror, it still didn't register that it was me. Never really had much thought at the time about what I saw. I just got into the bath, as normal. I was still really tender, and the movement of my left arm was still restricted, so I had to be very careful getting in and out in case I slipped. I couldn't put my left arm out to protect me. It's surreal really, hard to explain.

Jim made a lovely stew in the slow cooker. It was lovely. If nothing else, I'm getting well fed. After dinner, he went to see Peter. After that, he visited Ryan, with wee Miley's Easter gift. She's lactose intolerant, so instead of chocolate eggs, we get her a wee bunny, or a cuddly Peter Rabbit.

We had our stew when Jim got back from Ryan's. It was more like pea stew, there were so many peas in it. Potatoes were also in the stew. It was green in colour, weird! I think it was overcooked, and that's why it was a bit mushy. Listen to me, it tasted nice, though!

If Jim had left three-quarters of the peas out, it would have been nicer. I could only eat half of it. Jim gets really miffed if you criticise his cooking. He's a good cook, most of the time, but garlic goes in everything. He thinks what he likes, everyone likes. He always puts it on high heat, then it turns to mush!

I relaxed the next couple of hours, read my library book, and watched some TV. Left side of my body is still tender, as I said earlier. I'm told to put Bio-Oil on my scar, as it's known to be a great healer.

Nancy came up the next day and did all my ironing, not that I have much, just pyjamas. I'm wearing these days. Might start a new trend. You can get some nice ones; they look like lounge sets.

She's a godsend. You readers know what it's like when you're out of action, and you can't get your normal routine done, tidying up, hoovering, laundry, all those tedious things that need done around the house.

Jim's quite good that way, but you know, they never do it the way you do. We should be grateful. I am. And they bug you if you can't get things done, stupid, I know. As if, after breast cancer, a mastectomy, housework should be the last thing on your mind.

The brain does weird things to your head when it's been turned upside down with this diagnosis, and your routine has been abruptly changed.

Jim went to see his daughter Yvonne. She has an ear infection. Did I mention that she and her husband Mark are police officers? Her earache could be quite serious, dizziness and nausea.

I have had labyrinthitis a few times over the years. It's so scary, you have no balance and you are crawling on all fours just to go to the toilet. The only time I felt safe was when I was lying down on a bed or a couch. It can last for weeks.

Jim took Yvonne shopping later. Its good they're spending time together. It gives him a wee bit of respite from being in the house with me all the time.

Junior and Claire came to visit me with their young grandson, wee David. He's a wee cutie. He's not feeling too good, he has problems with his ears. He's only about 2 years of age. What is it with ears? Is there something in the air that's causing all these infections?

Our Nancy is going around the house making tea for everyone. She must be knackered, exhausted, but she never complains. We all rally around. That's what families do, you readers know that.

Jim bought Nancy a new trolley dolly. Hope she doesn't take it the wrong way! But it's to save her carrying all her shopping bags, as she would not take the money for getting our shopping. What is she like, eh? She's *some* woman, as Jim would say.

I just relaxed after our visitors left. You don't realise how tiring it can be, just sitting talking to people.

I woke up at 8 o'clock. Not sure how long I had been sleeping. I'm still taking the painkillers. I've read three books since coming out of the hospital. I love a good book, me. Jim got me one, it's a page-turner. I'll pass it on to my Claire. She is an avid book reader. It's all about biological stuff, she'll like it. She studied that at university.

I was wakened at 3:00 a.m. this morning. I was in so much pain. I took more painkillers and had a really restless night. You can't get comfortable. When you go to roll over onto your other side, your body jerks from the pain. You don't realise you're doing it, you're sleeping, obviously. I have propped up pillows, so if it happens, it won't be so painful, I hope not. I've written all that in my wee book.

Today I'm in a fair bit of pain. Jim took Jess out earlier. She's never left my side, that wee dog. She lies at the side of my bed; she's a wee cracker. They seem to sense when things aren't right, when something is different. They're so clever, dogs.

Argh! Only two painkillers left. I need to call the doctor for more. Nancy will collect them tomorrow for me. My chest feels so tight just now. The doctor says, 'It's the nerves knitting together.' Sounds like they're making a scarf. I hope there are no holes in the knitting.

I'm doing my chest exercises. Did I say they had to remove lymph nodes from under my left arm to check that the cancer hadn't spread there? They tested them, and they were alright, thank goodness. Not sure if I mentioned that earlier, sorry if I'm repeating myself. Under my arm is still really tender in that area. I can't wait to get the dressing off so I can see what it looks like. I want to look, and I don't want to look. I want to see what they have done to my body.

The tightness might go away when the dressing comes off. Who am I kidding? The tightness is coming from the inside.

Kirsty and her mum Janice are coming to visit tomorrow. I'm looking forward to seeing them. They have been there for Jim and me. Every one of the family has. We can't thank them enough.

Kirsty, Ryan, Colin, Janice, and wee Miley came to visit tonight. Wee Miley kept us going with her antics, she's so funny. I hadn't laughed like that in ages. Well, I had to control it a bit as I was still tender. I couldn't even give wee Miley a cuddle. I always lift her up and spin her around, but I couldn't do it tonight. She was pretending to be a teacher and telling us what to do, very official sounding she was. We were all rolling about in tears. Well, not literally rolling about, but you get the gist. I think that's the word for it. What a wee tonic she was for me.

I've been told my wound will be tender for a long time to come, maybe years. It will ease off eventually but will never completely go away. It will always be there, just not so severe.

Eileen and Emma are coming to see me tomorrow. Emma is a good friend of Laura's, and her mum and I are also good friends. Laura is coming to visit tomorrow after her shift at work, which finishes at 8 p.m.

Today is the day for my results. Nancy picked me up in a taxi. My appointment was for 11:30 a.m. I met Sheila there, she was the woman in the bed next to mine in the ward. She was called first, and when she passed me, she said, 'I'll speak to you later.'

My results were good. They said they got 84% of the cancer out. I then had to decide what treatment is best for me. I have to go for a bone scan, as the tablets they are putting me on cause your bones to thin. April 24th is the date for my bone scan. I get to speak to the oncologist then.

I was so tired when I got home. I don't seem to have much energy these days. I was so tired, I went straight to bed. After a couple of hours' sleep, I got up and got ready, well, not dressed. I was still in my pyjamas, for Emma and Eileen are coming up to see me.

Eileen and I had a good wee catch-up, I hadn't seen her in ages. Emma and Laura could talk for Scotland. Eileen said so, and I quite agree with her, Christ, I have a cheek! I'm worse than those two put together. My family say they can't get a word in when I start to talk. I think they're havering.

The time went by so fast, and it was time for them to go. I really enjoyed their company. I've known Eileen and her daughter Emma since they were at nursery. Laura and Emma joined nursey at the same time. I can't believe it's been that long, you wonder where the time has gone, and how fast it's flown by. You always get Eileen the same way, no matter where or when you meet her. Love her and Emma.

I woke up to Jim bringing me two sandwiches and sausage, or as we say in Scotland, two pieces "n" sausage. I ate and loved every mouthful. Next thing I knew, I woke up again and our Nancy was at the door. It was 2 o'clock in the afternoon! I must have been really tired to sleep that long. I must have needed that sleep.

They say, there I go again with 'they say', that you're healing while you are sleeping. I love all these wee sayings. Nancy made me scrambled eggs on toast. She makes the best scrambled eggs. I told her that, and she thinks I say it just to get her to cook them for me.

They broke the mould when they made Nancy, I kid you not. Jim's scrambled eggs are also good; he puts some cheese in his.

After Nancy went home, I massaged my scar with Bio-Oil. It's very red-looking, and the scar runs from right under my arm to the centre of my chest. I think I already described it earlier. It's raw-looking, and I don't know what to say, it looks weird. The space where the boob was is very flat, and there's a dent in it. At the very end of the scar, there's what they told me is called a "fish tail". It's actually like a very, very tiny wee boob, just about the size of your thumb. They told me to keep an eye on it, because if it gets bigger, it could be filling up with fluid, not so good. So I will definitely be keeping a watch on that. It's also still tender.

It might sound like I'm moaning all the time, but I'm not. I'm just trying to explain how I feel and to let you know how the operation and everything else went. I mean, if this information helps one person understand and know what lies ahead for them, then it's all been worthwhile. I know we are all different and heal differently, but it could be a wee bit of help somehow, I hope.

I called Claire and had a wee gab to catch up, then watched *The Graham Norton Show*. I like his show, he always has good guests, and he's so funny. I sat for a wee while after it finished, lost in my own thoughts. I should be tired, but I'm not. I'm off to bed now, I think it must be about 1:30 a.m.

I tossed and turned all night. I had a wee glass of wine to celebrate my good news, that they got most of the cancer out. Yeh! Brilliant! Best news ever! I called all the family and friends to let them know. They were all over the moon and relieved, like myself.

David is coming to visit me today at 3 o'clock. I'm looking forward to seeing him. I had a bath this morning. The wound still looks quite red. I'll keep my eye on it. I'm keeping up with my exercises, tough, but they have to be done, or the tissue and muscle will stiffen up. Maybe I'll go out tomorrow for a wee walk in the fresh air.

I didn't go for a walk today, didn't feel up to it. Nancy came up to see me and to check if I needed anything from the shops. She washed my hair for me, I still can't reach up to my head. She went home about 9 p.m.

I took half a sleeping tablet. You're probably thinking, *She's taking too many sleeping tablets*, but it's the only way I can get some sleep these days. I was on the couch, got up in a dreamlike state, must say, I had a good sleep.

Today it's Junior's birthday. Happy 70th Birthday, Junior! Usually Claire, his wife, would arrange a night in Oliver's for parties, but Junior was adamant he didn't want one. They're coming to visit me, then going for a meal for his birthday treat. I hope they enjoy it.

I'm getting the car valeted today. Nancy's also coming to visit. I'm certainly not short on visitors, she will need a holiday soon, with all the running around she's doing. Jim made Nancy and me a lovely pork dinner.

I washed my hair today, as it gets very greasy lying in bed most of the day. My breast feels tight today, well, I should really say my left side. There is no breast. Some days it's tighter than others. Dr Rousse is on holiday just now, not back until next week. I will call her then.

I'm trying to get cream for my scar. I've read you need to wait two to three weeks, not sure why. I'm massaging it gently, as they say this is good for it. I'm not really that interested in going out just now, maybe later.

I went to the doctor's; it was a locum. I felt like my scar looked infected. The doctor took swab tests to check for infection, which I hope I haven't got. That's all I need. I'm waiting for the results, maybe I'll get them Thursday. I was given antibiotics again.

Nancy took me to Morrison's for some shopping; first time I've been out apart from going to the doctor's. First time I've been shopping since this happened to me. I met Georgina, a lady I worked with in the Nutmeg Department. I get on really well with Georgina. She was really shocked when I told her about what had happened to me. She said, 'Carol, mind, if there's anything you need, let me know. I can bring shopping over for you.' That was so kind of her. I thanked her and said, 'I will keep in touch.'

I got up late the next morning, 10:30 a.m. I made baked rice, but I still can't get it right. My mother used to make baked rice for us kids, we loved it. The smell around the house was magic. No one made it like my mum did.

Dr Jenny called about the letter to exempt me from wearing a seatbelt while I'm driving, as wearing it would be too painful. I'm on my second day of antibiotics, hope they work this time.

I spoke to my Claire last night. She's back at work after her bout of tummy virus last week. I sent an email to Sheila to hear how she got on at the clinic. I've been tidying up a bit here and there, then I'll have a wee read of my book, *The Immortal Life of Henrietta Lacks*. Sheila says it's very interesting. I'll post it to my Claire; she will like it. I'm going to have a wee roast beef salad for my dinner tonight.

Nancy came by to take wee Jess out. We had a wee gab, then some gingerbread and butter. Good to ourselves, eh? We had a cuppa too. Laura came up to see me, we had a laugh. Jim is always winding her up, but she gives as good as she gets, sometimes even better! She is looking very well, is Laura. She's on this no-carbs thing, and I must say she looks really good on it.

Sorry, these things actually happened on Wednesday, wrong day. What am I like, eh? Again, as mentioned on the previous page, I had written down that Laura came up to see me. It was lovely to see her. I'm getting my days mixed up. Jim does wind her up, and she falls for it most of the time. It was the first time I'd seen Jim smile in a while. He's been so serious and down these days. I'm getting fed up along with him.

I'm trying to keep upbeat, as they say. Maybe he's just fed up coming home and seeing me in my PJ's every day, but I'm not getting dressed up just to sit in the house. What's the point? Plus, think of all the extra washing! I'm not going anywhere outside until I feel well enough. I can't wish this better, it's going to take as long as it takes.

I'm still trying to come to terms with what I have, if I ever do. Never mind the fact that I have lost a breast, a part of me, and trying to adjust to that. Everything else is on the back burner at the minute.

I got up early, 7:30 a.m., to call Social about my claim. Not that they are open at that time of the morning. By the time I got ready, had breakfast, etc., I was on the phone for nearly an hour. According to my wee bookie, this was yesterday I did this. I called again this morning at 8 a.m., the phone was finally answered at 8:40 a.m., only to be told I had to call another number, which I am still waiting to be answered.

It's bloody shocking, all that waiting. It's so frustrating, as you can imagine. No wonder the blooming country is going downhill, that's my opinion. And may I add, at last the phone gets answered… and then they proceed to talk over you. Great. I mean, you're calling them, you pay your bill, the least they can do is listen to you and let you put your case forward.

I would rather be working, honestly, than going through this debacle of a landmine, that's what it feels like. And not to mention the hurt on your ears with the ridiculous music they force you to listen to. I mean, who chooses that music? They must have never heard decent music in their lives. I would love to meet them and say, 'Hey! Try and listen to this music, Fleetwood Mac, Dire Straits, Elvis.' Would be pleasant on the ears, don't you agree, readers?

That's got to be better than the dross they're playing down the phone. It's not even good supermarket music, is it?

Dr Jenny is calling today about the results of the swab test that was taken the other day. It *was* an infection. Eventually got through to the Social people, it's like an interrogation, honestly.

Wait until you hear this, they said I might get sent for a medical in a few weeks to see if I'm fit for work. Eh? Excuse me? I think someone has crossed wires or provided false information. Something's not right. Are you having a laugh? I thought to myself, *is this really happening to me?* Is it all in my head or my imagination? Are the doctors imagining this too?

Oh, and I almost forgot, they asked me if I will survive more than six months. You couldn't make it up! What's all that about? And you're supposed to be recuperating! How can you, when all this is going on? Along with the examinations, appointments, stress, etc., let alone all the information you're trying to take in and make some sense of.

I ask you, what kind of people can do that job? It's horrendous, asking people those questions. There must be another way, surely. I know I couldn't do it, that's for definite.

I know someone's got to do it, but I feel like I'm repeating myself. Can they not show a bit of empathy? Or ask in a more delicate way? That's just how I feel. Maybe they are told to be upfront and not personal, they have to answer to their bosses. I should have put a complaint in, but at the time, I just wanted my stuff sorted out. I was taken aback when asked these questions, and the manner in which they were asked.

That's all. I'm not blaming the people who work for them, they have to earn a living. But the training could be miles better, or at least improved in their vocabulary.

Today I have to go for a bone scan at Yorkhill Hospital. My appointment is at 1:15 p.m. Jim is coming with me. He has taken time off work to be there for me. Jim met me there; I took a taxi from the house. After we came out, Jim went back to work. I met up with Nancy, and we went to the Deoch n Doris, a wee pub in Partick, where we had a lovely pub lunch. It was my treat. Nancy looked so tired, don't forget she is still working as well. I said she should go straight home and get a rest, but she wanted to take wee Jess out for me first. She has wee Garry, her grandson, staying over, it was his sleepover at Nanny's. She really needs a complete rest.

We had a domestic last night, Jim and I, and he's still not talking to me. How childish is that? Well, that's up to him. Honestly, men and their bloody huffs and mood swings! I really don't need the stress and anguish of an argument. How selfish I think he is being. I tried to talk to him, and all I got were one-word answers. So I said, 'Fekking grow a pair.' And I wouldn't be the only one to say that at this time.

As I said, he's not dealing with this, but shouldn't put his bloody moods on me. That's not my problem. I have more than enough on my plate. I need to use my energy for my own needs. I can't be a**** with that carry-on, life's too short for all that.

The mood swings, the silent treatment, the poor-me syndrome, for f**** sake, I'd rather he went to live in his own house. Jim and I don't live together, we tried it once and we didn't even last a week. No kiddin'. And that's me being honest. So maybe at this stage, he should go home. I won't say that to him, as he would feel really cut off and hurt. In his mind, he's doing a great job and would feel not wanted. He thinks staying here is helping me, but enough with the moods already.

Also, if the girls are doing something for me, I know he feels left out and helpless. I can tell by the look on his face. He says as much.

The next morning, I woke up at 9:30 a.m. I had a good sleep, as I had taken, no, not a wee wine, a wee tablet, a half. Don't worry, they are prescribed by the GP. Jim's still not saying too much. The atmosphere is awful. I hate it. I'm sitting in the bedroom watching James Martin, I love watching him cook. His programme is also good; he has good guests on board.

I heard the door closing, that must be him going out. He didn't say anything about going out. 'Goodbye,' I say. 'Peace at last.'

That's what I mean with this cancer, it does not just touch me; it touches everyone around me. It changes them, I think, well, some of them. Even some of my friends, they don't know what to say to me, for fear of offending and hurting me. I personally try to be the same old Carol. I try to have a laugh most days. There's nothing wrong with a bit of banter, I always say.

People who have things happen to them often joke about it. For instance, when my Claire dislocated her knee repeatedly, it happened so many times, we lost count, seriously, but Claire would crack a wee joke about it. She called it her "Gammy Knee", and other wee jokey things. That's what it was like for me. I would say stuff like, 'I had to give up my lap-dancing job because people were asking for their money back, saying they were short-changed as I only had one boob.' I mean, you have to laugh. I did.

Back to Saturday, I ran a bath for myself. Claire called earlier. She said I sounded a bit down. I was. I told her I was fed up. Shouldn't be complaining, I'm still here. I never told her that Jim and I had words. She would have been very angry with him, and I don't want any more hassle. The rest of the family would have been angry too. They would have had words with him, no doubt.

I went in for a bath. I felt really vulnerable but just got on with it. I was getting a little bit stronger every day. I felt better after my bath. Jim came home; he had gone to his house for a while. He didn't say much. I just put last night's pizza in the oven and watched TV. Later I went into my bedroom and watched Gordon Ramsay. Jim was watching something else on TV in the living room. Wee Jess looks as fed up as I do.

As if I don't feel bad enough already, I feel like I'm being punished for having this cancer, because having it has upset our routine. We were used to going out for meals, visiting friends, and going to parties. Well, excuse me, I never asked for this. You'd think the way Jim's behaving that he was the one who had the cancer and the surgery.

I'll say it again, honestly, men! I'm not saying they're all like that, but sometimes... REALLY!

Anyway, going back to when I was asked, 'Are you going to live more than six months?', it's in order for them not to give you more money than you should be entitled to. That says a lot for our Government, scared in case you get a penny more than you deserve, or as they say, your *entitlement.*

Oh God, that makes me so very, very angry. You're going through a mountain of paperwork, and it continues for months and months, for all different departments. You can easily get disorientated. I hope I'm not repeating myself and that I haven't already told you this, I don't think I have.

I was out in touch with a representative of Maggie's Centre, so I made an appointment to see a guy called Greg, and what a lovely guy he is. He is very understanding. He listened to how I felt and explained how all the forms and literature worked. I was there for about an hour and a half. It didn't feel like that though.

Greg helped me enormously, I can never thank this guy enough. A gentleman is what he is. I could never have gone through all those forms or even understood them and what they were all for. Greg said, 'Carol, call me anytime you need to go through letters, forms, etc., and any concerns you may have.'

Brilliant to know that someone has your back. It's a big relief, I'll say. He is only a phone call away, and I won't need to wait for ages on the phone or get moved to different departments.

I leave a voicemail, and Greg will get back to me as soon as he can. So, on we go, we plod along and get on with life.

Jim is still going to see Peter. God only knows how that's going, excuse the pun. I thought it helped at first, but now I'm not so sure. I think Jim thought this would have been done and over quickly. I'm not sure what his idea is about how long he thinks it takes. I get the impression that he didn't think it would drag on this long. Well, I didn't either.

I would love to shout, 'In fact, it's me it's dragging on for!' Jim can go out for a walk, run, or hide from this, he gets some respite. I don't. It's here. I have it. That's a fact. I can't walk out or hide; it comes with me.

So on we continue. To be honest, if this doesn't split us up, then I don't know what will. And if we hang on, then it will be a miracle.

Today is the anniversary of my nephew, Stephen. Sixteen years now since he has been gone. He was 29 when he passed away. We all miss him. He was the life and soul of any party that was held, would dance his way into the hall, saying 'Hi' to everyone. He loved to dance. What a guy.

He would have been devastated by my news and would have been there all the way for me. He would have even insisted that he came with me to the hospital, I'm positive of it.

Today is the first time I haven't been to the graveside, as I can't drive yet. And when Jim finishes work, he's on shifts, the cemetery will be closed. Hopefully I'll be better to go on his birthday, the 13th of June.

This breast seems to be getting tighter and tighter. The doctor says it's the nerves healing. I know, I keep saying that to myself. And by God, it's really itchy. More than usual. I'm putting calamine lotion on it, it takes the edge off, but it's still driving me nuts. And you try not to scratch.

Sometimes it starts during the night. You can't go to sleep until the itch eases or gets more bearable. It's actually itching now as I'm writing this. There's no warning, it just starts.

I had a few visitors today, Claire, Junior, and David. It's always nice to see them. I don't know where they get their energy, they are always on the go.

I sent a wee text to Nicole, it's her birthday. Scott and Tracey's daughter. How fast the years go by! I can remember when she was born. Christ, I feel old. As the young ones are getting older, so are the older ones. Like me,

Scott and Tracey also have a son, Scott. He's 18 I think, if not, then I'm sorry, Scott. I can't remember at the minute.

It's lovely and sunny today. Jim and I went for a walk down Crow Road. On the way back, we popped into *The Three Craws*, as you do, for a wee cider. We came back up the road, and I made lasagne for Yvonne, Mark, and Laura. They're coming up to visit.

Yvonne brought me lovely tulips and a six-pack of Scampi Fries. I *love* them, just a wee notion I have. I'll eat them for about six months, then I won't want to look at them for a long time. They also brought some toys for wee Jess and a cheeky wee bottle of Prosecco. What's not to like, eh?

Yvonne took some lasagne home with her. She said she liked it. Mark, her hubby, is a vegetarian. He took two Empire biscuits home with him. Laura stayed over.

Her scooter was disabled again. I love her company. As usual, Jim was winding her up.

I am sitting here, suitable for my needs. I think I overdid it last night. I'm feeling pretty tired today. Yesterday was my first proper day out. The weather helped a lot.

It's raining today though, what's new, you say? It's mostly raining in Glasgow. Everybody knows that.

Referring to my breast being missing, I find the bras and the prosthesis irritate my skin when I wear the ones they have in the stores. I break out in red blotches and little white spots, and it's very itchy to boot. This happens even when the prosthesis is tucked into the pocket of the bra. They don't all have these little pockets, but it comes in handy at times.

I feel very self-conscious when I wear them, and people know I have one on. I'm always saying to anyone that's with me, 'Can you see them?' I think they get fed up with me asking. They say to me they wouldn't notice about the prosthesis if I never said anything. I think they're saying that to make me feel better. No, they *would* tell me. I'm always saying, 'Am I horizontal? Are anybody's?' I mean, whose boobs are?

It's how you *feel*, as I've said before. Some people don't realise that and say, 'Och, you're fine.' The more you hear that, the more you think they are saying it just to please you. I understand.

My scar is healing okay, I think. It's still very, very itchy. The redness is fading a wee bit, and it's not so fiery looking. I showed it to my sister-in-law, and she thought it looked like there might be an infection there. I made an appointment with my GP at the surgery to get it checked out.

You're not going to believe this, do you remember the GP at the beginning of all this? She told me not to worry as it was only a "mouse breast". I couldn't believe it when I saw her! She had the cheek to say to me, 'Just as well I sent you for a mammogram.' I said to her, 'You told me it was a mouse breast! Turned out it was an emergency, as you see, I lost my breast.'

She didn't know where to look or what to say. She gave me a prescription for the redness. *She didn't think it was infected.* I took that advice with a pinch of salt. And she said to come back and see her if I had any problems.

I was feeling quite bitter towards her, I'm being honest here. There are psychological sessions I have to attend. They're to make sure I'm doing this for the right reason and that I am in the right frame of mind, or so they say. You go for these sessions every 5 to 6 months until they think you are ready for your reconstruction.

Up until now, I've been to four of these sessions, or meetings, whatever you want to call them. Maybe more than four; I can't remember, to be honest. They're long and tedious for me, and they bring back lots of memories, right to the forefront of your brain, about how you're feeling all over again.

Because of COVID, my operation, and I suppose everyone else's, has been delayed, cancelled, or pushed back until further notice.

I'm still waiting. After five years, I'm beginning to think it is my age that's stopping them from doing the reconstruction. I once asked my doctor if age was actually a reason, and he said no, as long as I was healthy. According to the last examination I had, the doctor said I was 'ready to go', as long as I keep myself healthy as I am now.

I feel selfish, as there are people out there who haven't been diagnosed yet because their appointments keep getting put back. They're still waiting for appointments and results and are stuck in limbo. But I am here. I am alive. I must say thanks to the wonderful surgeons, Miss Donague and her brilliant team, who assisted in my operation. I am eternally grateful to her. You bet I am.

The doctors always say, 'Call us if you are worried about anything'. But I have called them a few times, and they have said, 'Speak to your breast nurse', and it's been quite abrupt, I would say. I felt as if I was being shunted away. These wee things mean a lot to you when you're going through this cancer journey.

This might make me sound really selfish, like I have the "it's all about me" syndrome, but don't misunderstand me. When I have called them, they have always called me back. I shouldn't be mean to them. They have taken great care of me. The fact that I am even writing these notes, this book, or whatever you want to call it, I call it *my journey*. I am still here thanks to their care, science, research, and meds. A whole combination of things going on behind the scenes to help people like me survive this disease, and several other diseases they are trying to combat. It's a testimony to their dedication and care. I don't doubt that for a minute.

We are still waiting for any information about my reconstruction. Meanwhile, I attend the Gartnavel Cancer Unit every six months for a drip in my arm. A small price to pay, I say. The drip contains bisphosphonate to strengthen my bones, as the cancer tablet I am on thins the bones. You take one tablet to make you better, and another to counteract it. Confusing, isn't it?

I have a catalogue of hospital letters, but then again, they're keeping an eye on me. Nancy has come with me numerous times. She must be fed up going there. I don't blame her if she is. I made an appointment to find out how long it would be before I got my reconstruction. I got an appointment quite quickly and went to the Gartnavel Clinic. Of course, our Nancy came with me, which I was glad about. What a woman she is. I always say to her, 'I want whatever vitamins you're taking, you're always on the go!'

I got called into the clinic room. Miss Donague asked me why I made the appointment. When I explained it to her, she said, quite abruptly, I may add, 'Why didn't you get it done when you were getting your mastectomy?' I took, by the tone in her voice, that I was wasting her time. I know the surgeons are really busy, but I am a patient too. I didn't think I was wasting her time; this is my life I am discussing here. The *quality* of my life.

I explained to her: when I was told I had cancer in me, my first thought was to get it out. I wonder what she would have chosen if she were in my shoes. Anyhow, we were not there to discuss her health. Maybe, with hindsight, it would have been better to get it all over with at once.

But that wasn't my thinking at the time. I just wanted that horrible disease out of my body as soon as possible. And I also thought, 'What if I get this reconstruction, and later find there is still cancer inside me?' Then they would have to go back into my body to get it out. That's why I opted for the mastectomy first.

I was told at the time that I didn't have to make a quick decision and could get the reconstruction at a later date. I explained all this to Miss Donague. She said she would put this forward to the surgeons, and that was that.

There was a neighbour of mine, a good few years back, who stayed upstairs from me. He was a medical student then, a very young man, and a good neighbour. His name was John. I met him in the hospital on one of my visits. He had recently qualified and was now a doctor. He said, 'What are you doing here?', as it was in the breast clinic. When I told him, he was really shocked and said how sorry he was. He asked me the name of my surgeon. When I told him, he said, 'Oh, the formidable Miss Donague.' Now what does that say to you? It says a lot to me.

I remember one time in the ward, the day after mine and Sheila's mastectomy. Miss Donague came striding in. The vision of Miss Trunchbull came to mind. If you have ever seen the movie *Matilda*, then you will know exactly what I mean.

She went right over to Sheila's bed, pulled the curtain back, and said, 'How dare you put DNR on your consent form?' I mean, that is Sheila's, or any other patient's, choice. She continued to say, 'If I thought you weren't capable of having this operation, I wouldn't have proceeded with it. You undermine my ability.' Poor Sheila looked like a five-year-old getting scolded for stealing a cake. And what if Sheila didn't want anyone to know? I mean, that was personal information!

Sheila said to her, 'No, I had every confidence in you.' Miss Donague then asked how she was, and Sheila said she was fine.

Then she walked over to the bottom of my bed and asked me how I was. I said, 'I am fine.'

I was dreading her coming nearer to my bed and asking questions. She marched out the ward like a soldier on a mission. We were dreading her coming to the ward on her rounds. We said we would hide in the toilets. Can you picture that? Sheila and I, two patients with their hospital gowns on, drips hanging from our sides, we would have got caught because we couldn't stop laughing. Seriously, we were hysterical. Knowing me and Sheila, that would have been a sight to behold.

As I said before, *Frenchie*, my name for Sheila, when I first saw her and spoke to her, I knew she would be a tonic to me. Truly, she was, and she still is.

The nurse would come around the ward to ask if we needed painkillers. I would always say 'yes', but Sheila would refuse. I thought to myself, *Gosh, she's really a brave woman.* No painkillers? I was eating them like sweeties, not really, but I was taking them when I was offered them.

Unbeknownst to me, as Sheila told me later at one of our many coffee mornings that we arranged afterwards (we meet regularly, well, as often as we can and still do to this day, and hopefully always will), the reason she didn't take painkillers was that she had her own herbal medicine. It helped her more than the tablets the nurses were giving her.

On our first coffee morning, she took me to *The Western Baths* in Byres Road. She is a member there, so I didn't have to pay, as I was a guest. She took me on a wee tour of the place. It's been there for years, since the Victorian era. It's quite a nice place, old-fashioned, but that adds to its quaintness. I would like to find out more about it from Sheila.

Her husband bought her the membership as a Christmas gift. Do you know they have a trapeze swing going over the swimming pool? I would love to go on that! I was mesmerised when I saw the trapeze at the circus and always wanted to have a go. Imaging swinging on that, then dropping into the water! I haven't said that to Sheila, knowing her, she would arrange it for me. I might say it to her one of these days.

Years ago, it was only men who were allowed in these premises, like a lot of these establishments. It's all changed now with these rules, and for the better, I think. Well, now not only ladies but children also are allowed. Also, they have a small restaurant, so you can have a workout, a lovely swim, and then a lovely lunch.

Sheila and I always have a right good laugh when we are out together on our coffee mornings. She tells me about her friends and the antics they got up to, and I tell her mine. This is really a tonic for both of us, recovering from this dreadful disease and trying and get back to normal living.

She is a very intelligent woman, and the places she has travelled to! I will tell you about them another time. I mean, she travelled to Egypt in the sixties. She was only 21 years old then. She was 82 going in for this operation when I met her. She's 85 now, and still working! What an inspiration she is to me and to everyone else.

I am writing this because it may help other people to think, *Well, if this lady Sheila can do this at her age, then there's hope for me.* The morning after our operation, she was up with the lark, as they say, in for a shower before I had even rubbed the sleep from my eyes. No kidding, she put me to shame.

She once said to me, 'Hey Carol, I wonder what the going rate for a one-breasted woman in the circus would be?' I couldn't stop laughing at her saying that. That's what I mean by her wicked sense of humour, we were always able to laugh at ourselves.

She went back to her job after her convalescence. I'm not sure how long after the operation it was. She would always say to me, 'Carol, they didn't have much to take from me. That's how I'm healing faster than you!' What is she like, eh?

Sheila is a tour guide. She takes American tourists all over Scotland. She loves her wee job. I really admire her, I take my hat off to her. I don't have the energy to go to the shops on my own. It's great we met when we did because it gives us a chance to talk about how we are healing and any queries we might have. And it's the connection, that we are going through this together. We understand, it's not like talking to someone who hasn't a clue what it's like, only what they read in books. It's not the same.

I once said to Sheila, 'I can't stop looking at other females' breasts, walking up the road, in cafés, everywhere. I feel like a weirdo.' She said she was the same. It must be a thing that mastectomists do, that's the name I've made up for us.

I've started going out a bit more, to the supermarket and Braehead. I wear my bra and prosthesis, but not all the time. Sometimes I go out without it and hide that side of my body with my arm, holding onto my shoulder bag.

I would forget sometimes and try on a coat or jacket, and I would see people looking at me, Our Nancy would say, 'Never mind anybody else, what you have gone through, you just be comfortable and don't feel awkward.' So, as I said, I started going out more, even wee nights out now and again, as my energy was getting a lot better.

I was always checking myself to make sure the boob was in the right place, the prosthesis boob, I mean. I had to make sure the prosthesis wasn't moving around too much. Sometimes it'd travel to the centre of my chest, making it look like I had three boobs! Some of these bras, as I have said before, don't have a wee pocket in them. Also, if I wore a V-neck top, I just had to bend over, not that much, just slightly, and you could see the gap where the boob once was. You have to be very careful about what you wear.

That's why I used to get annoyed when I was getting ready for a night out or for a shopping trip, nothing would look right. You're a female, we want to look attractive and sexy and feel like a woman. As we all know, ladies, don't we?

Nancy calls me the Return Queen, as I don't try anything on in the shops for fear of someone might open the curtain and see me. I wait until I get home and try them on there. I feel better doing it that way. Hence why I sometimes have to return things, which is about nine times out of ten. It doesn't bother me, but our Nancy says she couldn't be bothered with all the palaver, as she calls it.

Only having one boob, it's nothing compared to the fact that I am still here, thank God, and enjoying life. I'm going through my bucket list as I go along. I'm always checking my right boob, and I get a mammogram every year instead of every three years. I just want them to look normal under my clothes, as normal as they can be.

Anyhow, back in the room, as they say, there I go again. Who are these people that say all these things? They seem to say a lot, don't you readers think? We are always quoting them. The appointments keep coming in, to the different medical units:

radiologists, mammograms, staff, psychologists, doctors, and nurses. I have been put on a waiting list for reconstruction. They said it could take three to four years. Up until now, I've been waiting five years, and counting. I personally feel they have forgotten me. Or, it's what I thought, it's my age. That's the barrier.

They say it isn't, but I beg to differ. The doctor says if there is a cancellation, then I would be called and maybe get it quicker. In the meantime, I have to keep myself as fit and healthy as I can. But with all this damp weather, it's not so easy.

Some of my friends are saying, 'Why don't you just leave the reconstruction?' I know where they're coming from, but it's how you feel that matters too. When I look in the mirror and see my breast missing, then I really want the reconstruction. But the longer time goes on and I don't hear any word about it, the more I feel like, *Oh, just forget it. I'm not getting it anyway.*

I'm not sure how people who are disabled feel, how they cope with missing limbs, etc. God love them. I think I know how they feel. I keep reminding myself, *I'm here, so just get on with it, and I do.*

I have resigned from my wee job in Nutmeg. I was absent from the job for a while after my operation. I don't have the same mobility down my left side as I had before, with the lymph nodes being taken out.

The Area Manager paid me a visit to my house. You know, you feel as if they don't believe you and they have got to come and see for themselves. Really it doesn't do anything for my confidence. She suggested I go in for a few hours at a time. I mean, there are heavy pallets to move around, and I'd have to try and hold onto three to five pairs of skirts or trousers on hangers. The weight all adds up. They can get quite heavy when you're walking around the store trying to find out what rail they belong to.

It would take me ages, and I know myself, I would get very frustrated that I couldn't do the job the way it should be done, or the way I did it before I became ill. It wasn't practical for me to return to work at that early stage.

The Area Manager came to see me a few times, and the answer was always the same, I wasn't fit enough for work. Finally, they accepted that I wouldn't be able to return. I liked my wee job and felt I was contributing to something, the community, or whatever, but I was doing *something,* and it gave me confidence, working on my own. And through no fault of my own, I had to claim benefits, something I never did in the past, as I've worked since I left school at 16, until this happened to me.

My brother and sister-in-law, mind, I said they live in Spain. I went over there; it was six weeks after my operation. I asked the doctor, and he said it would be okay. Claire, my daughter, came with me. We booked for a week. I was thinking the sunshine might help with my recuperation.

Boy, how wrong was I.

I was struggling with the pain and the whole thing altogether. I realised then it was far too early. So why did the doctor say it would be fine? I thought I was coping well, but I wasn't, really. We came home three days into the week's break. I was so relieved to get back home. I think it was because the hospital was just up the road from me. I felt safer being home. I wasn't so far away from help if I needed it.

My brother and sister-in-law both felt I was struggling, and they said so later when they texted to check how I was keeping. So much for a wee break in the sun, but it wasn't to be.

Anyway, there will be other times to go for a wee break in the sun when I am a lot stronger. I was really exhausted when I got home. I think the travelling and everything else took a lot out of me. I hope it has not set me back. I wrote in my wee book: *I was trying to do things too early*. I realise that now.

What I needed was lots of rest, not gallivanting off to Spain. I think I got caught up in a nice idea and just went with it, without thinking, *What if something goes wrong?* As I said, I felt okay when the doctor said it was okay. I should have thought about it more. I really should have.

I hope that reading this will help anyone who is going through cancer. I'm hoping that it will give them an insight into what's ahead for them. It may not be the same as what I went through, but it might give you a heads-up, and you may not be so scared and frightened of the unknown. That's the worst part of it: going into the unknown, not knowing what's in front of you.

The information I have provided through my own treatment will hopefully help you. Your mind can work overtime, and you imagine all sorts of things being wrong with you. You always fear the worst. And you can make yourself ill, feeling nauseous, stressed, and anxious. Your anxiety levels can go sky-high.

I know, I felt the same. When you're told for the first time, you think to yourself, *'I'm going to die.'* It's only natural to think like that. Then you think, *What about my children? What about my partner? What about my husband, my family, and my friends? Will they cope?*

The bottom line is, they *have* to step up. And so do *you*. Sorry to be so blunt, but there's no hiding place.

It will be worse if the children are very young. I can only say: tell them as soon as you can, before they hear it from someone else. It's better coming from you. You can reassure them. Children are very resilient, and they will surprise you with how they can cope.

Always be honest with them. If you're in pain, say so. Don't hide it. They only want to help, so don't shut them out. They want to be there for you. These are things I found that helped me, so I hope they help you in some way too.

Well, that so far is my journey through cancer. And I'm still waiting for my reconstruction. So that will be another part of my journey.

I'm not sure if I told you my age? I was 63 when I got my mastectomy. That was five years ago. I think, as I said earlier, my age is against me, although the doctors say that is not the case. So, I'm still waiting. (Another song, Diana Ross!) Personally, I hope it won't be too far away now, and I can tell you all about *that* journey.

Please, all of you take care. And if you find a lump or anything different in your breast—shape, size, colour—please call the doctor. Because I'm still hear talking to you, *because*

I didn't hang around, I got an appointment right away, and I caught it early.

I know it's scary, and you're scared to find out, but it's better to know than sit and worry yourself sick.

Hope to speak to you all soon, and tell you about my new boob.

Bye for now.

I wouldn't have got through this without my wonderful family and friends. You know who you all are.

Thank You.